ARMS A KW-480-511

ARMS AND ARMOUR
1660 to 1918
The Soldier and his Weapons

G. A. Shepperd

With illustrations by Isabella Whitworth

Rupert Hart-Davis London

Granada Publishing Limited
First published in Great Britain 1971
by Rupert Hart-Davis Educational Publications
3 Upper James Street, London, WIR 4BP

ISBN 0 298 79144 7

Printed Offset Litho by
Cox & Wyman Ltd, London, Fakenham and Reading

Acknowledgments

The Author wishes to acknowledge with grateful thanks the
valuable help given by the following:
The Ministry of Defence Library (Central and Army); the
Imperial War Museum; the Royal Artillery Institution; the
Institute of Royal Engineers; the Scottish United Services
Museum; the Royal Armoured Corps Tank Museum and
the Armémuseum, Stockholm.

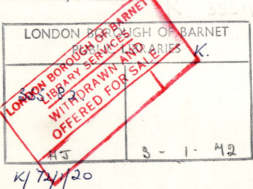

Contents

To my Grandsons
Alastair and James

Chapter One

The Soldier King

The saying 'a man's home is his castle' reminds us that in feudal times the castle, with its garrison of men-at-arms and stores of weapons, food and water, provided the ultimate defensive stronghold and refuge for the whole community against aggression. On the battlefield heavy cavalry, exemplified by the knight protected from head to toe in elaborate and often costly armour, had dominated the scene for over three centuries. As late as the sixteenth century, riding into battle encased in several hundred pounds of steel, they had remained largely immune from the elementary weapons of the foot soldiers, whether it be the bolt from the crossbow, the long-shafted arrows of the English archers, or the almost universal halberd or pike. Today, in an age which in some twenty-five years has seen the development of rockets that can carry men on journeys of thousands of miles into outer space, it seems strange that 200 years should have passed between the discovery of gunpowder, recorded by Francis Bacon in 1249, and the fall of Constantinople in 1453, when the Turkish artillery successfully breached the most formidable fortifications in Europe in forty days. A few years before this latter date the French guns of Charles VII had forced the surrender of sixty English strongholds in Normandy

Gun versus Castle; sixteenth century

in a single year. Before the development of siege cannon each of these fortresses would have taken up to twelve months to reduce by assault or starvation. Towering walls of stone no longer gave protection to the garrison, and fortifications soon became adapted to resist the solid shot of the siege batteries. Broad earthworks with low ramparts, protected from direct assault by a wide ditch often filled by diverting the waters of a nearby stream, were built with embrasures for fortress guns sited to cover the approaches and keep the enemy at a respectful distance. Meanwhile the increasing efficiency of firearms, in the form of the arquebus and later the musket, slowly but inevitably changed the whole pattern of warfare. The common foot soldier now had a weapon that could penetrate the heaviest armour that man and horse could carry. The day of the knight in armour was ended and a golden age of cavalry was passing. These developments, improved firearms and more mobile artillery, soon brought changes in military organisations and tactics. The most revolutionary of the changes were due to the genius of Gustavus Adolphus, King of Sweden and creator of the first modern army. The innovations which he introduced are of particular interest because they were soon adopted by many other countries and changed the whole pattern of conventional warfare.

Musketeer versus Horseman

In the early part of the seventeenth century cavalry were still the most important and numerous part of an army, and the only one capable of manœuvre in battle. The wearing of heavy armour had virtually been abandoned and mounted men had adopted fire-arms as their principal weapon. Shock tactics were now rarely used by the cavalry except when the musketeers were re-loading. In battle array, bodies of musketeers were generally placed at the corners of a dense phalanx of pikemen, as each was dependent on the other, but this mass of foot soldiers often lacked training and discipline, and was incapable of man-œuvre, or of proper defence, except to their immediate front. The ponderous cannon employed in the field, whether for the siege of a fortress or in a set-piece battle, were served by civilian artisans, who often belonged to a special guild of cannoneers and were engaged for the duration of the campaign. When an army was drawn up in battle-order the guns were usually massed in the centre and out in front. The cavalry and infantry of European armies were made up of mercenaries who were enrolled into what were called trained bands. Their loyalty depended on regular pay rather than on any national allegiance or religious scruple. The soldiers were accompanied by hordes of camp followers, with whole families following the fortunes of the men-at-arms; and sutlers, who were itinerant tradesmen, went from camp to camp. No attempt was made to set up magazines or stores, and the whole army, including the numerous hangers-on, lived by indiscriminate pillage. Strategy thus depended more on the capture of a well-stocked town or the occupation of a rich agricultural district than on the movements of the enemy. The move of an army into winter quarters often resulted in the unfortunate local population being reduced to starvation point through the seizure of all their crops and livestock.

When Gustavus went to the aid of the German Protestants in 1630, during the Thirty Years' War, he was only thirty-five years old, but he had been campaigning in defence of his country since he was seventeen. To defend its frontiers he had been forced to fight on foreign soil and advance first into Poland and then into Germany. Against the Poles, who had many mounted men, he had learned the value of mobility. But Sweden was a poor country that could neither raise nor afford a large cavalry force. So Gustavus saw that he must create a new kind of army with cavalry, infantry and artillery moving and fighting as one force. He decided that the mobility of the whole army depended on training and discipline and that discipline depended on good administration.

Gustavus introduced a system of conscription. Any man with no settled occupation was automatically enlisted and ten per cent of the male population of Sweden between the ages of eighteen and thirty were chosen by lot for national service as foot soldiers. This raised about 15,000 men, but the nobility and their personal servants, who were exempt from service as

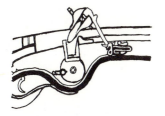

Wheel-lock

Paper Cartridge

foot soldiers, provided the nucleus of the mounted regiments. Such was Gustavus's reputation and success that within two years of marching to the aid of the German Protestants he was commanding a force of 50,000 men. The Swedish national army now contained many foreign recruits and half of the King's infantry consisted of Scottish and German contingents. The army received regular pay and in enemy territory supplies were obtained through a properly regulated levy on the civilian population. Looting was forbidden and camp followers were not tolerated. Officers were given ranks and were chosen according to their ability, regardless of nationality or social standing in their own country. Uniforms were adopted for the various units and initially these merely consisted of scarves of various colours. These innovations brought a sense of team spirit and dedication that enabled Gustavus to insist on strict discipline without recourse to inhuman floggings.

Pikeman; early seventeenth century

Gustavus based his tactics on increased mobility, fire power and aggressive action. The musket became the chief infantry weapon and a gradual change-over was made from the matchlock to the flint wheel-lock. The musket itself was shortened and lightened so that it could be fired without a rest. The bore was now based on twelve balls to the pound weight. Instead of the clumsy bandoliers and jangling charge cases, paper cartridges, complete with charge and wad, were

11

carried in pouches slung over the shoulder. This reduced the number of movements necessary for reloading, as the musketeer simply bit off the end of the cartridge and rammed the charge home. Consequently fire power was greatly increased, and battle formations could be made more flexible. Relieved of carrying the rest, each musketeer now carried a sword, and his defensive armour was reduced to a pot helmet. Two-thirds of the infantry were musketeers and the remainder were pikemen. The armour of the pikemen was reduced to a cuirass and thigh pieces and they carried either a sword or a battle-axe. Their pikes were shortened from sixteen to ten feet and could now be held with one hand. To receive a cavalry charge the Swedish pikeman held his pike in a slanting position with the left hand, steadying the butt against the right foot. This freed the right hand to use the axe or drawn sword. All the Swedish infantry were practised in forced marching, and carefully trained to carry out a number of battle manœuvres, as well as being thoroughly drilled in the use of their weapons.

Gustavus organised his infantry into small units with a high proportion of officers, as he was determined to achieve a proper system of command and manœuvre on the battlefield. Each company was about 125

Wedge formation

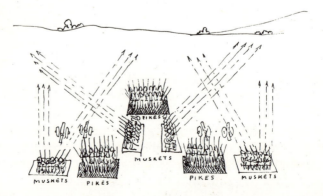

men and had a normal strength of 72 musketeers and 54 pikemen. Four companies made up a battalion of between 400 and 500 men. This battle group, as it would now be called, was easily manœuvrable and much less vulnerable to artillery fire than the inflexible, solid phalanxes of several thousand men that had been adopted by the Spanish and other Continental armies. A regiment consisted of three battalions, and a group of several regiments formed a brigade. Gustavus trained each regiment to deploy into a wedge-shaped formation with the pikemen divided into three bodies, the centre one being pushed forward to make three limbs of a cross. The musketeers were posted in the gaps of this loose formation so as to cover the front and flanks of the pikemen, and if necessary, cover the rear of the formation as well. When the army was drawn up, the brigades themselves were formed into two lines with intervals between the regiments, so that the second line could move up into, or through, the gaps of the first line. Unlike their opponents, the Swedish pikemen formed only eight deep and the musketeers six deep. As soon as action was joined, the musketeers formed into three ranks: the first kneeling, the second stooping, and the third standing to fire. This avoided the constant movement of platoons to the rear to re-load, which was the general practice in other armies. The musketeers were also trained to fire volleys by all three ranks simultaneously. Delivered by competent and disciplined troops, and at close quarters, these volleys proved devastating to cavalry and foot soldiers alike.

The Swedish guns were still served by civilians, but under the command of army officers, and now were standardised into three types: siege, field and regimental pieces. To achieve mobility, the weight of all three types was reduced. The siege guns weighed up to about 6,700 pounds, and the field guns between 1,350 and 3,000 pounds. The regimental piece, a 4-pounder, weighed only 560 pounds, and could fire either shot

12-pounder cannon; early seventeenth century

or grape. Mounted on a special carriage, the regimental guns were particularly mobile and could be drawn by a single horse, or three men. Two of these regimental pieces, which were a thousand pounds lighter than those in other armies, were allotted to each regiment. The gunpowder charges were prepared in advance as cartridges which were boxed up, so as to be easily carried and immediately available. The result was that the field and regimental pieces could fire three rounds to every two that were fired by the enemy. This innovation of prepared charges was also considerably safer for the gunners who previously had had to collect the charge from an open gunpowder barrel. Other Generals often concentrated their artillery in front of the centre of their army, but Gustavus spaced out his guns along the whole of the battle front, in the same way as his cavalry was interspersed with his infantry. All three arms, or parts of his army, were thus complementary to one another.

Since the heydays of the heavily armoured knight, cavalry tactics had completely changed. The lance had been abandoned. Carabineers or dragoons, named after the short muskets they carried, advanced at the trot making half wheels and other manœuvres to draw the enemy's fire. When sufficiently close they performed a caracole, that is to say successive ranks fired and then turned and filed off to the rear. Hand-to-hand fighting would only follow after their opponents had been sufficiently disorganised by this fire. A few armies maintained bodies of cuirassiers, armed with pistol and sword, but these were only used against troops already thrown into disorder by gun or musket fire. Gustavus appreciated too well the value of the speed and weight of the horse to imitate these tactics, and his cavalry was trained to charge at speed and rely on the keen edge of their swords. His cuirassiers were trained as heavy cavalry, or in other words, as shock troops, but were lightly armed and equipped. They wore a helmet and breast-plate and carried two pistols and a long sword. The dragoons were trained as light cavalry. They wore no defensive armour, and carried a musket and a sword. The dragoons were also trained to fight on foot, but this was not their primary role. Being so lightly equipped they were very mobile and could act as mounted patrols to keep the enemy under observation. Each Swedish cavalry regiment was about 560 men with eight troops of 70 men each.

The cuirassiers were rarely committed in the opening stages of a battle and Gustavus often held back a body of infantry in reserve as well. This of itself was a new departure as the custom in other armies was to advance *en masse* at a slow pace and not to hold back any reserves to throw in at the moment of crisis. Gustavus's favourite method of attack was to soften up his opponents' closely-packed battle formations with a heavy cannon-ade. Then, launched through the gaps in his own infantry and screened by the clouds of black and acrid smoke that hung over the battlefield, his heavy squadrons rode forward at a fast pace straight at the opposing infantry. The troopers of the first two ranks were trained to discharge their pistols only when they could 'see the whites of their enemy's eyes', and then to draw their swords and engage hand to hand. The third rank rode straight into the *mêlée*, each man with a pistol in either hand, holding their fire until the last moment. Then they too drew their swords. The whole charge was made at speed and was followed up by the Swedish infantry who rapidly moved forward to shatter the enemy by volley fire and to hold the gains achieved by the cavalry. With the enemy thrown into confusion, the Swedish cavalry, which had re-formed, then charged into the flanks of the broken formations, usually with decisive results.

King Gustavus was killed at Lützen in 1632 in a battle that showed the complete superiority of his small, disciplined units over the great massed squares of 3,000 infantry adopted by the Imperialists. Many of his innovations were copied in other armies, and in particular, by the French. With the abandonment of huge massed squares of infantry, the Swedish wedge-shaped formation also dropped out of use and regiments were invariably drawn up in linear formation.

The New Model Army formed by Thomas Fairfax and Oliver Cromwell during the English Civil War in 1644 owed much to the influence of Gustavus. Formed as a permanent force, it consisted of 11 cavalry regiments, 12 infantry regiments, and 1,000 dragoons and totalled 22,000 men. The infantry were organised into small, mobile units, and the proportion of musketeers to pikemen was two to one. Each troop consisted of 100 men. Armed with sword and pistol they were trained in a manner similar to that of the Swedish drills.

Musketeer; early seventeenth century

On the Royalist side, Prince Rupert, who had served with the Swedes, trained his cavalry on similar lines, but as a Commander he proved to be over-impetuous and unable to control his men once they had been launched in a charge. Cromwell's Ironsides, as his heavy cavalry were called, and which he himself trained and led, were better disciplined and charged in close order at 'a round trot'. Furthermore, Cromwell always kept a reserve in hand and this, combined with his ability to control his men in action and make quick decisions, enabled the Ironsides to play a decisive part in the major battles of the Civil War.

Chapter Two

Rise of National Armies

THE FLINT-LOCK

By the middle of the seventeenth century the expensive
and rather delicate wheel-lock had largely been replaced
by the snaphaunce lock. This mechanism originated in
Holland and was copied in many other countries. A
schnapphahn was a Dutch chicken thief, but the word
also meant a pecking rooster or cock and this exactly
describes the action of the flint striking down against
the steel to produce a shower of sparks above the flash
pan. Snaphaunce firearms were very much cheaper
to make, costing only about a quarter of the price of a
wheel-lock, and stood up better to rough and ready
usage. The pyrite that produced the spark in the wheel-
lock often crumbled and the wheel housing and driving
chain had to be kept free from fouling. A flint, however,
lasted for about twenty shots before it had to be changed.

The Italian snaphaunce lock has several features of
the true flint-lock. The cock is in the firing position,

Snaphaunce lock

and when the trigger is pressed, the end of the sear is pushed up releasing the tumbler so that the cock is thrust forward by the mainspring. At the same time the lever pushes the flash pan cover away to expose the priming powder. Thus, when the flint strikes the roughened face of the steel, sparks fly straight down to ignite the priming powder and the flash passing through the touch hole fires the charge. A small spring holds the steel in position ready to receive the glancing blow that produces a shower of sparks in the pan below. When the snaphaunce was loaded and primed it was carried cocked but with the steel raised and pushed right forward to avoid an accidental discharge. Being more reliable, snaphaunce pistols were in common use for cavalry but there were still hundreds of thousands of matchlock muskets stacked in arsenals and armouries all over Europe. These were issued to the infantry for reasons of economy, and continued in use for a number of years. The obvious disadvantage of the matchlock musket, however, encouraged armourers everywhere to seek a strong and simple flint-lock mechanism which would be cheap to manufacture in quantity.

The invention of the true flint-lock, in about 1610, is attributed to a Frenchman, Marin le Bourgeoys, and the earliest known example of his invention, later called the French lock, is on a magnificent gun in a museum in Leningrad. Since the steel and pan cover were all in one piece, there was now no need for a special mechanism to push back the pan cover, and the priming powder was protected from the elements as the steel always remained in the forward position. An important de-

French lock

velopment was an extra-deep notch on the tumbler which enabled the cock to be held in a 'half-bent' or half-cock safety position. The cock was pulled right back before firing so that the sear engaged the smaller notch. As an additional safety device a dog catch was often fitted on the outside of the lock.

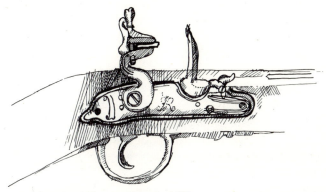

English flintlock or carbine c. 1680

From a 'General state of all the Ordnance' in the British Army for the years 1687–91 we find the following listed: 'Matchlock and snaphaunce musquetts, snaphaunce dragons, carbines ordinary (of 2 feet, 7 inches) and long (of 3 feet), pistols, blunderbusses and musquettoones.' The dragons had the same bore as a musket, but a barrel only sixteen inches long. Like the blunderbusses and musquettoons they were usually issued to the Navy or for some special service or guard duty, where a lighter, and more easily handled, firearm than the musket was required. Carbines which were also known as fuzees or fusils (hence the term fusilier) were lighter and smaller in bore than the muskets of the period. In 1679, we find that Prince Rupert's dragoons were issued with 'twelve fuzees and sixty-eight muskets with slings', cartridge boxes and bayonets. In the same year one of the newly formed grenadier companies was issued with 'fuzees with slings, cartridge boxes with girdles, granadoe pouches, bionetts and hatchets with girdles'.

THE BAYONET

The evolution of the bayonet is closely linked with the improvements in firearms just described. Musketeers, armed with matchlocks, had invariably been given the protection of pikemen against a cavalry charge while engaged in the lengthy process of re-loading. At close quarters they used their swords, or more often swung their heavy muskets to club their enemy down. Although for the remainder of the century matchlock muskets continued to be used in large numbers (in the British Army up till about 1690), flint-lock muskets were being produced all over Europe in increasing quantities. In the hands of disciplined and trained men these lighter and more easily handled muskets and fusils brought a gradual change in the organisation and tactics of the infantry as a whole, which now came to rely more and more on fire power. Less and less pikemen were used and in the British Army they were finally abolished in 1702. Unencumbered by the heavy matchlock and its rest and the whole paraphernalia of bandoliers, bullet bag, and match and priming horn, the musketeer, armed with a flint-lock, was certainly more mobile, but when it came to hand-to-hand fighting he had to rely on his sword. If he was armed with a fusil this was provided with a sling so that he could move and wield his sword more freely. Volley fire might check, but could not halt, a determined cavalry charge, and against opposing infantry sooner or later the field must be won by closing the enemy. Although pikemen were out-moded, there was still need in close combat for a thrusting weapon.

The first use of the musket to serve both as a firearm and to hold a thrusting blade had been tried out as early as 1647. The practice had arisen of soldiers adapting their hunting knives or daggers so that they could be plugged into the barrels of their muskets. At close quarters, after a volley had been fired, the plug bayonet was a useful weapon, and because of the weight and length of the musket, it was often far more deadly than the sword. The handles of plug bayonets were sometimes made of ivory or horn but usually they were of plain, varnished wood with brass quillons and ferrule. Originally, these bayonets had a blade a foot long and a handle of about the same length, tapered so that it would fit into any size of barrel. An obvious disadvantage was that the handle had to fit tightly, as otherwise the bayonet could be knocked out, or even left in the body of an opponent; and of course the musket could not be reloaded while the bayonet was fixed. The solution seemed to be to fix the handle on the outside of the barrel by two rings, but this never worked satisfactorily because there were so many different sizes of barrel and the rings tended to work loose. In 1671, however, the French invented a bayonet with a socket that fitted round the end of the barrel so that the musket could be re-loaded and fired with it fixed. The 'split' in the socket enabled it to be altered so as to fit the different-sized barrels. This bayonet was first used by the French against the British during the campaigns fought by William III in Flanders. The adoption of the socket bayonet led to the final abandoning of the pike and a revolution in infantry tactics.

Plug bayonet

Socket bayonet

GRENADES

The use of grenades dates from long before the invention of gunpowder. Earthenware or glass vessels filled with quicklime, or incendiary material, were hurled by hand and often used in sieges. Since the second half of the sixteenth century grenades were manufactured of cast iron and looked like a cricket ball, but with a filling hole so that the powder could be poured in and

21

Grenadier c. 1670

a fuse inserted. Special grenadier companies were formed of men 'dexterous in flinging hand granados'. These elementary hand grenades were carried in a large pouch. The grenadiers themselves were picked men of good physique and stout heart as their role needed a cool head as well as a strong arm. There was not only the danger of a premature explosion but grenadiers were invariably detailed to lead the attack on a fortress or the storming of a trench. To enable them to sling the musket more easily over their shoulder, they were issued with 'furr'd caps with coped crowns like Janizaries which made them look very fierce', instead of the customary wide-brimmed hat.

Various means were tried out to increase the range. The most successful method evolved was by fitting a cup or discharger to the muzzle of the musket. The grenade was placed in the cup and at the appropriate moment the fuse was lit. The musket loaded only with powder was then fired in the direction of the enemy. This was altogether a rather clumsy business and highly dangerous if the flint-lock misfired. An extraordinary combination weapon of this period, made by John Tinker in 1681, may be seen in the Tower of London. This has a cup discharger built into the butt which is hinged so that the musket could also be fired in the ordinary way. There is a special spring trap on the flash pan that allowed either charge to be fired separately. A hinged steel rest permanently fixed to the stock steadied the whole contraption while the grenade was being aimed and fired.

Tinker's combined grenade discharger and musket

Finished cannon

ARTILLERY

Warlike stores of all kinds, from cannon to accoutrements and tents, were the province of the Master
General of Ordnance, and it was he who decided by an
'ordinance', or regulation, the specifications of each
item. In the case of cannon, the vital statistic was the
calibre or size of bore. Guns in general were known as
pieces of ordnance. In earlier times particularly large
pieces of ordnance were given names, such as Mons
Meg, still to be seen at Edinburgh Castle, and Sweet
Lips, which was a great piece of ordnance used at the
siege of Newark. The development of artillery was very
slow. The pieces were all muzzle loaders and, except
for the very small and relatively ineffectual field guns,
were so large and clumsy that once dragged into position they could not be moved quickly. Cannon were
mounted on a heavy, wooden-wheeled carriage. Mortars had to be fired from a 'bed' placed flat on the ground
and were mostly used in sieges. The other kind of piece
in use in the early days of artillery was what we would
now call a howitzer. This was a short piece mounted
on a wheeled carriage; like a mortar it had a high
trajectory. All types of ordnance were made of bronze,
but some cannon were cast in iron and these were often
used in ships' guns. The difficulty of using cast iron
was to avoid air bubbles which weakened the barrel.
The special names, such as Royal (8-inch bore), cul-
verin (5 inches) and falcon ($2\frac{3}{4}$ inches), given to various
sizes of cannon persisted, but they gradually became

23

known by the weight of the solid shot that they fired, 24-pounder, 12-, 8-, 6- or 3-pounder.

The manufacture of cannon needed a good deal of skill and patience if anything like a regulation bore was to be achieved. A replica of the barrel was built up from a mixture of earth, powdered brick, hair, and horse dung, round a centre core of timber called a truss. The truss was set up on trestles, and by turning it the profile of the gun could be shaped by hand tools. This full-scale model was then dried hard by a slow fire. The trunnions and handles, which were often shaped like dolphins, together with various ornamentations, were then added, being moulded in wax or carved out of wood. This solid replica of the finished article was then rubbed over with tallow and covered with several layers of a kind of putty composed of horse dung, potter's clay and hair. This outer layer was then 'bandaged with iron bands' and given another covering of earth. The truss was knocked out and the inner mould burned away. The breach-piece was formed in a similar way, and the two moulds wired together. The complete mould was then buried upright in a pit close to the furnace where the molten metal was being prepared. The bore was formed by securing a bar of iron, which had been covered with a 'paste of ashes bound with

Manufacture of cannon

French field artillery c. 1675

wire and thoroughly baked', exactly in the centre of the mould. The molten metal was then poured in.

When the metal was cold the cannon was dug up and the mould cut away. Rough surfaces were filed away and a touch hole bored into the breach. After this, the gun was 'proved' by firing different charges to see how strong it was. The cannon was then fitted on its wooden carriage, where it was held in position by the trunnions. Wooden wedges were used to adjust the elevation of the gun for various ranges, but it could only be aimed by using levers on the trail and wheels of the carriage and slewing the whole carriage round.

Mortars were mounted at a set angle of 45° and the range was determined by the amount of the charge. It had been the practice to fire a mortar in two operations. The shell, which in its simplest form was an over-sized hand grenade, was loaded on top of the charge. After

(a) Fireball   (b) Canister shot

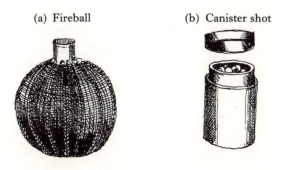

Thundering ball, with small grenades inside

the fuse had been lit the mortar was then fired through its touch hole. During the Siege of Limerick in 1691, however, an artillery subaltern hit on the simple expedient of allowing the fuse of the shell to be ignited by the flash of the discharge of the mortar itself. This was a good deal safer for the gunners and also allowed them to fire 'at will', instead of immediately after the shell was loaded.

Round shot for cannon were of stone or iron, but canister shot was often used against infantry. These latter were tin, wooden or even canvas cases filled with nails or musket balls. Amongst the innumerable types of projectiles mentioned by contemporary writers was the 'thundering ball'. This consisted of a hollow, spherical wooden case filled with hand grenades. Fireballs were reinforced canvas bags (made like a football) and filled with a highly combustible mixture, such as 'meal powder and coal sprinkled with brandy or oil of petrol', which ignited when the gun or mortar was fired.

The train of artillery which accompanied the British force to Flanders in 1694 provided sixty guns and six mortars. The Colonel in command had a headquarters staff which included a kettle drummer, whose pair of drums were handsomely mounted on a travelling carriage complete with coachman. There were four companies each with three officers, two Gentlemen of the Ordnance (who were storekeepers), and a hundred gunners and matrosses. The train was completed by the addition of over two hundred men for engineering and maintenance tasks. These included 'bridge and tin boat men' with equipment for making pontoon bridges (using some of the latest copper boats), carpenters, coopers, wheelwrights, collar makers (for repairing harness) and over fifty pioneers. One of the principal non-commissioned ranks was that of Chief Firemaster who was in charge of the mortars and the preparation of the various fire bombs and other special projectiles

26

Mortar and shells

used in sieges. The drivers for the various gun teams and the wagons that carried all the power and shot and other paraphernalia were all civilians.

SWORDS

Nowadays in Britain, swords are only worn on ceremonial occasions, and then only by officers, sergeant majors and the Household Cavalry. Three hundred years ago, however, every soldier carried a sword as an essential part of his personal equipment. An officer had to buy his own sword in the same way as he had to provide his own uniform and accoutrements, but in the case of the other ranks, the sword and belt were issued with the uniform that was provided by the Colonel of the Regiment. The cost of the sword, however, was recovered through a stoppage of pay known as 'off reckonings' and on discharge the soldier kept his sword and belt. So long as armour was commonly worn, swords tended to be long and heavy, and used for a sweeping blow. In the latter part of the seventeenth century the cavalry sword was very similar to that still carried today by the troopers of the Household Cavalry when they mount guard in Whitehall or ride down the Mall on ceremonial occasions. The blade was thirty-five inches long, but had no real thrusting point, and

Cavalry sword

27

Infantry
hanger

the sword was still heavy and clumsy. In the days of
Charles II, the infantry carried a lighter sword which
had a straight and rather narrow blade, and often a
simple cross hilt. This was called a 'tuck'. Later a
slightly curved sword with a shorter blade, called a
hanger, was introduced for grenadiers. The blade was
twenty-five inches long, and the hanger was considered
a better weapon for hand-to-hand fighting. Both of
these infantry swords were designed as thrusting
weapons. On the Continent some Hussar regiments
were being raised, and these carried a curved sword
with a very sharp cutting edge based on the scimitar
used by the Turks. Sword scabbards were made of
black leather and had steel mountings.

ARMOUR

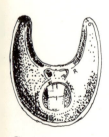

Gorget

Only the minimum amount of personal armour was
now worn. There were two kinds of headpieces in
general use. Pikemen wore a basinet which was often
called a pot and looked exactly like a pudding basin
with a rim. The cavalry wore a skull-cap made of thin
iron which fitted into the crown of their hat. Both pikemen and the heavy cavalry wore the cuirass which was
a back-plate and breast-plate joined together. After
the pike was abolished this type of armour was still
worn by the heavy cavalry, or cuirassiers, but was given
up by the remainder of the cavalry. Although the
wearing of elaborate personal armour was completely
out of fashion, General Officers, for some time, continued to dress up in it before a battle—presumably
as a symbol of high command. One piece of armour that
survived right up to the nineteenth century was the
gorget—from the French *gorge*, meaning throat. Originally designed to protect the neck-bone and collar-bone,
the gorget continued to be worn as a badge of rank by
officers when on duty. A captain, for instance, wore a
gorget of gilt, and an ensign one of silver plate.

28

CAVALRY

The cavalry of all the European nations were either cuirassiers or dragoons. In the English Army under William III, the Horse, as the cuirassier regiments were known, were armed with sword, carbine and a pair of pistols with 14-inch barrels. The carbine was fitted with a slide and a ring so that it hung on a belt worn over the left shoulder. The sword was slung from a cross belt over the other shoulder, and the cartridge case fitted on to a waist belt. A troop of Horse had a captain, lieutenant, cornet, quartermaster, three corporals, two trumpeters and fifty troopers. Three troops made a squadron and two or three squadrons a regiment. Dragoons were armed very much like the infantry with matchlocks, long straight swords and bayonets, and they often fought on foot. At an earlier period each troop had included some halberdiers who were really

French dragoons 1695

mobile pikemen. In 1687, however, the English dragoons carried 'snaphaunce muskets, strapped with bright barrels, of three feet eight inches long, cartouche-boxes, bayonets, granado pouches, buckets and hammer-hatchets; also good, broad cutting swords with three-barred hilts'. The buckets were fixed to the saddle to hold the musket. The hatchet served as an axe to clear the way in an advance, or as an entrenching tool, and even as a close combat weapon. Dragoon regiments that particularly distinguished themselves in action were granted the privilege of wearing their sword and carbine belts crossed like the Horse regiments. Instead of trumpeters, each troop had 'one drum and one hautbois' (the old name for an oboe).

Louis XIV spent enormous sums in raising and equipping an increasing number of cavalry regiments. Apart from many regiments of dragoons, the French Army now included several kinds of light cavalry who fought with sword and pistols and only carried a pro-portion of carbines for use in guarding the rear or holding a defile. Louis XIV also raised a special regiment of over 400 officers and 3,000 men as carabiniers. These had large swords, pistols and rifled carbines. The men carried two sizes of ball: one that had to be rammed home with a mallet, and the other much smaller and made for rapid loading. When the tight-fitting ball was fired the carbine was of course much more accurate. A number of Hungarian deserters were also recruited into the French Army as hussars. These splendid horsemen were mounted on small, but fast, horses of great endurance. Using very short stirrups, and crouched low over the necks of their mounts, they charged at a gallop in a loose formation, each man wielding a heavy sabre or battle-axe. Lancers were used in both the Polish and German armies, but needed to be backed up by cuirassiers. Except in the case of these two specialised types of cavalry, the carbine and pistol dominated cavalry tactics. Manœuvring became more and more deliberate to enable all three ranks to fire a simultaneous volley, after which the charge was made at the trot.

INFANTRY

The adoption of flint-lock muskets did not happen overnight, and it seems that at least one pattern of flint-lock musket must have proved unreliable as the Coldstream Guards were issued with fusils in 1660, but five years later changed back to matchlocks. This was the period when a third of the infantry still carried pikes. Most musketeers were armed with the tried and trusted matchlock and a sword, and were equipped with bandolier, ball bag and priming flask. The pikemen also wore a sword with a shoulder belt, a pot helmet and back-plates and breast-plates. Under William III's influence, however, the English infantry became the

French infantry, 1695

a. Officer's partizan

b. Sergeant's halberd

c. Sergeant's pike

best armed in Europe. Most foot regiments were now armed with flint-locks, swords and bayonets. Each battalion had ten to twelve companies, each commanded by a captain with two subalterns. The establishment for the company was: three sergeants, two corporals, two drums and a hundred private soldiers, but in peace-time this strength was often allowed to drop to half this number. Each battalion now included a grenadier company for which the tallest and smartest men were chosen. Grenadiers also had to be of good physique to carry much heavier equipment than the ordinary infantry soldiers. They carried a fusil with sling and had always been issued with a bayonet. Later on, they also carried a hanger. Cartridge boxes were worn on a girdle, and a pouch full of grenades was slung over one shoulder. Finally, as they invariably led the assault on a fortress they also had to carry a hatchet. An innovation was the forming of fusilier regiments equipped with a lighter-weight fusil with sling, cartridge boxes, sword and bayonet. Pikes were never issued to fusiliers or grenadiers and by the end of the century this weapon had been abandoned. Officers all carried swords but officers of the grenadier companies also carried a light fusil. Other infantry officers were armed with a pike or partizan, and field officers, that is to say colonels or majors, carried a half pike.

FORTIFICATIONS

For two centuries the Italians had been the leading authorities on military engineering. In the seventeenth century their system of fortifying a town or military stronghold was to surround it with broad earth ramparts faced with stone. At regular intervals, strong points in the form of bastions were built out from the ramparts. These were in reality battery positions. Covering the bastions and the ramparts was a broad moat beyond which was the glacis—an even wider earthwork sloping

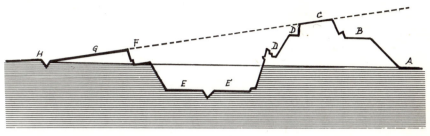

Section of a fortification c.1670

a. Level of fort	c. Parapet	e. Fosse or moat	g. Glacis
b. Terre plein	d. Chemin de rondes	f. Parapet	h. Outer fosse

away at such an angle that the guns in the bastions could sweep the glacis and the open ground in front. Between the moat and the glacis was a 'covered way' which had no overhead cover, but was a road running below the lip of the glacis that enabled musketeers to reach any sector that was threatened. The musketeers could then man the counterscarp or firestep and fire down the slope at any attackers. If forced back, the musketeers withdrew by plank bridges across the moat, or by tunnels underneath, to the main ramparts. This concept of broad earthworks and a series of reinforced battery positions, sited for mutual support and giving oblique fire across the sloping face of the glacis, was a recognition of the increasing effectiveness and accuracy of siege artillery. It was, however, a young French engineer officer who developed and perfected these ideas and became the recognised authority on forti-fication and siege methods for nearly two centuries. As a young man, Marshal Sebastian de Vauban had taken part in many of the sieges at the end of the Thirty Years' War, and made full use of this practical experi-ence. A man of boundless energy and considerable intellect, he had joined the French Army as a cadet at the age of seventeen and served as an engineer-officer for over fifty years. He designed, or reconstructed, the fortifications of over 150 strongholds—fortresses such as Lille and frontier towns like Strasbourg— as well as

33

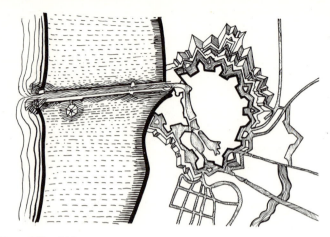

Plan of Dunkirk

laying out the defences of the French ports from Dunkirk to the Spanish frontier.

Vauban paid great attention to the lie of the ground
and where he saw a weak spot, which gave an attacker
the advantage, he constructed advanced strong points
to give depth to the defence. One of his innovations was
a detached strong point called a hornwork which was
built with two half bastions pointing towards the likely
line of attack. Other strong points were sited in the
moat, and these were either triangular or oblong in
shape, and called demilunes or tenailles. One of Vauban's
strongest forts was Neuf-Brisach in Alsace-Lorraine,
built to guard a bridge over the Rhine. This was a
self-contained town, with every possible amenity for
the garrison, constructed as a fortress and only completed after his death in 1707. It took ten years to build,
cost over four million livres and in design was the
last word in Vauban's methods of fortification. Its
design included all his innovations such as tenailles,
hornworks and redoubts, as well as bastioned towers
which mounted guns on two levels.

Fortresses were built with mathematical precision.

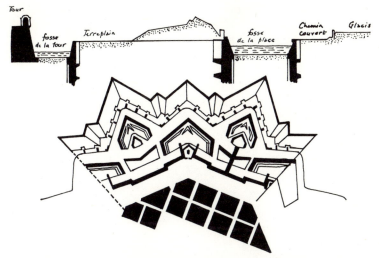

Plan of Neuf-Brisach with profile showing the double moat and towers.

The length of the courtine, which was the face of the rampart between two bastions, was always determined by the effective range of musket fire. Similarly, the positioning of the bastions was determined by the need to cover the approaches with the fortress guns which had a maximum range of about 2,000 yards. The bastions themselves were very strongly built and the guns were set in deep embrasures to give them the maximum protection from the attacking artillery. Each fortress gun could only have a narrow arc of fire, if it was to be protected in this manner, so several guns had to be mounted in each bastion. The task of manning the lip of the glacis and the various detached strong points was given to the musketeers. Their role was to prevent an infantry assault reaching the moat, if the attack could not be broken up by the fortress guns. In the last resort the garrison had to man the ramparts and try to prevent a breach being stormed.

Vauban also introduced entirely new tactics in conducting a siege. Hitherto approach trenches had been dug in a zig-zag manner to avoid direct fire and enable the attackers to get close enough to make the assault.

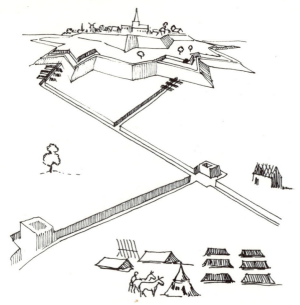

Attack of a fortress, from *Les Traveaux de Mars* published in 1672.

Vauban's method was to dig a series of trenches parallel to the line of the fortifications. A number of communicating trenches were dug forward from each parallel so that the work on the next parallel could proceed simultaneously at a number of points. The trenches were carefully sited so that the third parallel was within assaulting distance. All this was supervised by Vauban himself whose knowledge of fortress construction enabled him to calculate the distances and angles that would give his troops the best possible protection until the moment for the assault. The siege guns were carefully sited so as to bring fire to bear on several parts of the fortress. When the third parallel was completed the attacking infantry could assemble under cover, but the besieged garrison would still not know exactly where the attack would come. Meanwhile, Vauban's siege guns had been pounding away at the defences and there were several instances of the garrison surrendering

36

rather than face a strong infantry assault that might come from almost any direction. Such was Vauban's reputation that Louis XIV often made special journeys to be present at the final phase of a siege. A contemporary writer describing one such occasion at the Siege of Namur in 1692 wrote that 'Vauban avec son canon et ses bombes a fait lui seul toute l'expédition' (Vauban with his cannon and bombs himself carried through the enterprise), and in less than sixteen hours Vauban's troops had captured the enemy's covered way with its palisades, had filled in a moat sixty feet wide and eight feet deep and captured a demilune between two bastions, all for the loss of only thirty men. The French gunfire had been so deadly that the outworks of the fort were found to be full of dead bodies. The attack was now directed against a concealed fort covering part of the courtine where a desperate stand took place. Concentrated gunfire by the French artillery, however, forced the garrison of the fort to surrender, and soon afterwards the citadel fell to a strong infantry assault.

Although the defences of Namur were then greatly improved by Vauban, the Allies with a strong British contingent under King William re-took the town three years later. Over 185 guns and mortars paved the way for the assault, and the siege, which lasted for sixty-six days, cost the garrison 8,000 men. In the final assault the Guards suffered very heavy losses and the Royal Irish displayed such conspicuous gallantry that for the very first time a British regiment was granted a battle honour to be borne on their colours—in this case the words, *Virtutis Nemourcensis Praemium* ('Reward for Bravery at Namur'). The earlier Siege of Namur had lasted thirty-six days, on eight of which torrential rain had stopped all operations. If Vauban's advice had then been taken an entrenched camp would have been built close by for a counter-attack force and Namur might never have been re-captured. Although the fortresses built by Vauban were immensely strong (one

37

of them on the Belgian frontier held out for fourteen days against the Germans in 1914) no one knew better than he what an attacker could achieve by concentrated gunfire followed by a carefully planned assault by determined infantry.

THE RISE OF NATIONAL ARMIES

Earlier in the seventeenth century the maritime nations had been engaged in colonial expansion both in Asia and America. In Europe, as the result of the Thirty Years' War, the military power of Spain had been broken and some small states had been swallowed up or forced by the larger powers into coalitions for mutual protection. Extended home frontiers had to be guarded and the extra revenue needed for this had to come from overseas trade. These circumstances created a vicious circle. Without the wealth that came from overseas expansion a strong army could not be maintained to protect the home frontiers or indeed to guard the overseas territories. Both these tasks required a regular force of fully-trained soldiers who could take the field at any time. Since the training of a soldier could take up to five years, he was regarded as valuable national property and he was recruited for life. Gone were the days of raising troops by levy for a single campaign, and of living off the country. The improved weapons and equipment were not only expensive but difficult to manufacture quickly, so arsenals for the manufacture of the latest armaments were established and magazines were built to hold reserves of warlike stores of all kinds. Frontier towns were fortified and given permanent garrisons, and military roads were built to enable reserves to assemble more quickly. While from a strategic point of view much attention was paid to the building of defensive strongholds, commanders in the field became adept at manœuvring their armies so as to threaten their opponents' supply lines and only accepted battle under the most favourable conditions. The regular soldier was regarded as too valuable to be thrown away in an ill-conceived head-on collision. This new concept of manœuvring against an enemy's lines of communication and forcing him to leave his entrenched camps was much practised by Henri, Vicomte de Turenne. As the leading tactician of his day, Marshal Turenne became the successor of Gustavus Adolphus, and after his death in 1675 his policies were brought to fruition by Louis XIV's war minister, the Marquis de Louvois. A proper system of supply under a Quarter Master General's department was set up, and the whole army was organised on the permanent basis of brigades and regiments. A uniform standard of training and discipline was enforced by inspectors appointed by the King, and the name of one of these, the first Inspector General of Infantry, Colonel Jean Martinet, has ever since been a by-word for the enforcement of rigid discipline.

TACTICS IN THE DAYS OF LOUIS XIV

In tactics a revolution had taken place. The introduction of the socket bayonet meant there was now only one kind of infantry. This of itself simplified battle formations and tactics. Musketeers could now re-load and face cavalry without the protection of pikemen and they could also protect themselves when rain or wind restricted firing. Line formations in three ranks, which facilitated volley fire, became normal for both infantry and cavalry. Consequently the battle line became more extended. For instance, a French battalion of 600 men now occupied 200 yards of front, and as the size of armies increased so did the space taken up on the battlefield. Three-quarters of the troops were now infantry. These fought in the centre of the line with the cavalry holding the flanks. The tendency was still to concentrate the artillery in front of the infantry, but the guns had to be more spread out. No longer did armies crowd into a mass opposite each other, with the sergeant majors literally pushing the untrained men into position, rank by rank, with their halberds. The troops now had to be taught to carry out their arms drill and each manœuvre on the word of command or beat of the drum. Each manœuvre, such as forming line to face a particular direction or forming a hollow square against a cavalry charge (a drill movement perfected by the British), had to be performed 'from the march' and with absolute precision so as to leave no gap. Another essential drill was the opening of the ranks in the face of gunfire and their closing before joining action. All such manœuvres had to be practised until they became completely automatic, so that in battle, when casualties thinned the ranks, the line was still formed as if on the parade ground. Armies still formed up in two lines some 300 yards apart, but occupied such a large area that the peculiarities of the ground became important. Natural obstacles and the defence of key positions had to be studied, and cavalry had to reconnoitre the enemy's positions and discover how he was holding the ground. Turenne decided that the real objective was not the strongholds and fortresses but the enemy's army itself. By marching and manœuvring he forced his opponents out of their entrenched encampments to fight in the open.

The adoption of line formation and use of regular soldiers affected battle tactics in two ways. The battlefield became less of an arena, being chosen more for its physical features. Rivers and forests obstructed movement, and high ground gave dominant fire positions. Earthworks, consisting of trenches and breastworks, and palisades of sharpened wooden stakes were now used to improve the natural defences of any extended battle line. Equally, the higher standard of training of the regular troops enabled manœuvres to be carried out on the battlefield that would have been

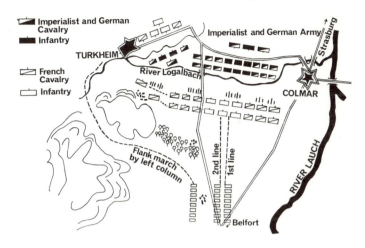

Imperialist and German Cavalry
Infantry

French Cavalry
Infantry

TURKHEIM

Imperialist and German Army

Strasburg

River Logalbach

COLMAR

RIVER LAUCH

Flank march by left column

2nd line
1st line

Belfort

French Army under Turenne
advancing in three columns

Battle of Turkheim

quite impossible in the days of the massed squares of mixed pikemen and musketeers. These movements, however, were performed with a deliberation that matched the formality of the parade ground where the various drills had been taught. Turenne studied both these concepts, the use of ground and of manœuvre, and realised that to achieve surprise they should be applied long before the first shots of an engagement were fired.

At the battle of Turkheim in 1675, Turenne was opposed by a force of 35,000 Allied Imperialists and Germans who had taken up a position behind a river line on a front of about 4,000 yards. The French Army (15,000 foot soldiers, 13,000 cavalry, and 30 guns), moving in three columns, was still some miles away when Turenne sent one of the columns, a third of his force, by a concealed route to attack the extreme right flank of the Allied line. This attack was a complete surprise and forced the Allies to withdraw under cover of darkness and abandon an otherwise strong position. If the flank attack had been reinforced, or the frontal

41

attack pressed harder, the French victory would have been decisive. Later, this kind of manœuvre was called Grand Tactics, and in Turenne's carefully thought out deployment of all three arms to make the best use of the ground we see the beginnings of modern warfare.

Chapter Three

Great Captains

Although in the eighteenth century the size of armies increased and wars were more numerous, the period is often described as one of limited wars. The leading states of Europe, with the exception of Britain where Parliament could control expenditure on the armed forces, were ruled by absolute monarchs who maintained standing armies officered by the aristocracy. In one sense, the army was an essential prop for the throne, set between the ordinary people and their ruler, who saw himself as a benevolent despot; and in another sense, the army was the accepted tool for furthering the political and economic ambitions of the state. Economic expansion was based on what was called mercantilism. The assumption was that the amount of wealth in the world was constant. This led to a long series of wars designed to seize the colonies and trade of another state by force of arms. This process was accelerated by a number of inventions such as those connected with the smelting of iron and the introduction of steam engines and of machinery for spinning and weaving cloth. Merchants, manufacturers and the armed services became increasingly dependent on each other. Yet each war had only a limited objective and the ordinary people were less involved than hitherto.

Soldiers lived a life apart from the civilians. Armies

One of Marlborough's infantrymen

became more and more self-sufficient, using large numbers of draught animals to move equipment and baggage. Campaigns were limited to those months when green forage was freely available. The scope of operations also was limited by the system of supply of food and matériel. This was based on magazines set three days' march apart, thus avoiding the need for foraging parties which could lead to desertions. Soldiers were enrolled for life and many countries resorted to drafting peasants into the army. Vagabonds and jail-birds who could gain a pardon by enlistment filled the ranks alongside foreign mercenaries who were found in every army. Desertions in the Prussian Army were as high as twenty per cent each year and raiding parties were sent into neighbouring countries to kidnap suitable men to make up the deficiencies that the draft could

44

not fill. Feared and despised by the community as a whole, the common soldier lived in isolation, and his welfare received little thought. This attitude was reflected in the scant attention given to any kind of improvement in his weapons and equipment, except in the matter of uniforms which could reflect the power and prestige of his royal master. Indeed, for the majority of the eighteenth century, soldiers served as the 'toys of Kings'.

Standing armies were expensive to maintain and the training of recruits, who lacked both education and any incentive other than fear of their officers, took a long time. Consequently, there was a tendency to avoid a battle that was likely to result in heavy casualties. With armies restricted both as regards size and employment and with few developments in weapons, there was a premium on generalship. Some improvements in weapons and equipment, however, deserve our attention before we discuss the tactical innovations of the great captains of this age.

THE BROWN BESS

By the beginning of the eighteenth century the flint-lock musket was in common use and it remained in use in every European army for 150 years. In Britain it became known as the 'Brown Bess', after the German 'büchse', meaning a gun. In fact, Germany exported flint-lock muskets, as well as the component parts, to many countries including Britain. As there were no factories for mass production, contracts for muskets went to gunsmiths in such centres as London, Birmingham and Dublin. These local craftsmen had for generations been producing private and sporting firearms but the size of the barrels varied and very often the socket bayonets did not fit properly. There were two early patterns of the Brown Bess. Both weighed between ten and eleven pounds, which was about the maximum

Brown Bess
and bayonet

45

the soldier could carry, together with all his other equipment, on a long march when he had to fight at the end of it. The first pattern was a graceful weapon with a 46-inch barrel. This was eventually superseded by a similar musket with a 42-inch barrel. When the Napoleonic Wars broke out, towards the end of the century, a cheaper and more easily manufactured Brown Bess, made for the East India Company, was issued in large quantities. This had a 39-inch barrel. The bore of the Brown Bess was about three-quarters of an inch and took a bullet weighing sixteen to the pound, compared with the French musket's twenty-four bullets to the pound. The socket bayonet had a triangular blade of about seventeen inches. In Europe, and particularly on the open plains of Flanders, the Brown Bess proved an ideal weapon. Its mechanism was simple, it was strongly constructed, and above all, it was easy to load. At forty to fifty yards' range the disciplined volley fire of the British infantry proved deadly. It was only later, in the fighting in America, that a lighter weapon with increased range was needed. The greatest virtue of the Brown Bess was the speed with which it could be loaded. The bullets used were one-twentieth of an inch smaller than the bore of the musket. Even after the barrel had become fouled with firing, the cartridge was easily pushed home, and with a clean barrel only a tap from the ramrod was required to seat the bullet firmly on top of the charge. Trained men could fire five shots a minute. This rate of fire was nearly twice as fast as most Continental infantry could achieve with muskets loaded with tight-fitting bullets that had to be laboriously rammed home. When firing into closely formed ranks at seventy or eighty yards' range accuracy counted for little, and the extra volleys fired by the British infantry, before the battlefield became obscured by smoke from the coarse black powder, often proved decisive.

EARLY RIFLES

There is a lot of difference both in range and accuracy between a smoothbore gun and a rifle. In the first place, when a rifle bullet leaves the muzzle, it is spinning and on this account has a more stable and accurate flight. In modern terms this is an application of centrifugal force. The spin is caused by a series of spiral grooves, called 'rifling', which are cut into the bore of the firearm which has now become a rifle. If the bullet also fits sufficiently tightly to prevent gases escaping when the charge is fired the muzzle velocity of the bullet is increased and so is the range.

Many parts of Europe used to be densely wooded, and abounded with wild boar and deer and other game that were hunted for food and sport. Sporting guns in Germany and Switzerland had been manufactured with rifling since the beginning of the fifteenth century, and contemporary woodcuts show huntsmen and members of 'sharpshooters' guilds taking part in shooting matches and firing at targets set at 200 yards' distance or more. No smoothbore musket, however well made, could possibly match this performance, and soldiers were taught to hold their fire until their opponents were within fifty yards, or less. Although the practical advantages of a rifled barrel were obvious, the ballistic principles were not understood until they were expounded in 1742 by an English scientist and Member of the Royal Society, one Benjamin Robins. Discounting an early belief that a spinning bullet had magical properties connected with witchcraft, one theory had been that it 'drilled its way' through the air. Another theory was that the grooves in the bore of a rifle acted as a brake to the initial movement of the bullet, thus allowing more time for the full force of the explosive charge to build up. Consequently, the practice had been to use an iron ramrod and heavy mallet to hammer an oversized ball down the barrel to ensure a tight fit. The result, however, was that this hammering distorted the

47

bullet, gases escaped and the flight of the bullet was erratic. Robins showed that to avoid the escape of gases and achieve the correct spin the bullet must fill the grooves cut into the bore. The simplest way of ensuring this was to load the ball through the breech and avoid the distortion from hammering with an iron ramrod. Various mechanisms were tried out, such as a barrel that could be unscrewed, or a breech which hinged open. Another idea was to fit a screw plug into the breech through which the ball and charge could be loaded. These mechanisms, however, wore out quickly and became dangerous, and were certainly too expensive to manufacture for military purposes. So huntsmen continued to use the time-honoured method of hammering the ball home and, to make sure of bringing down their quarry at the first shot, the size of the bullet was increased. These large-bore, muzzle-loading rifles had tremendous stopping power and were sighted up to 300 yards, but sometimes weighed as much as twenty-two pounds. When these massive rifles were taken to America by German or French emigrants they were found to be much too heavy to be carried on the long treks through the virgin forests of the frontier regions. The answer was found in the famous Kentucky rifle that will be described in the next chapter.

ARTILLERY

Throughout the eighteenth century there were few developments in artillery except experiments with small-bore, lightweight cannon that were sufficiently mobile to be manœuvred with the infantry and, if possible, keep up with the cavalry. Leather guns had been used extensively by Gustavus Adolphus. These had a copper barrel bound with wire and then covered with leather that was sweated on, being first well soaked and then allowed to harden. They were mounted on a light carriage, and very mobile, but they wore out very quickly. It is doubtful whether they were much used after about 1631, when at the Battle of Leipzig some of these guns got so hot that the charge exploded spontaneously with disastrous result to the crews who were loading them. The problem was really a question of weight and of evolving a suitable carriage. Small brass cannon were cast with a short barrel and were then mounted on light, spidery carriages with two small wheels (about 26 inches in diameter) and a light trail carrying a box for the canister charges. These became known as 'grasshopper' guns because when they were manhandled across country they bounced about in a crazy kind of dance. They remained in use, however, for about a century. The real need was for horse-drawn guns that were sufficiently light to keep up with the cavalry. Carriages were constructed with wheels of larger diameter, and a trail in the form of shafts for a horse. If the weight was kept down and the balance correct, the horse could gallop the gun forward into position. These 'galloper' guns were the forerunners of field artillery, and the German version fired an 8- or 4-pound shot. The introduction of horse artillery is attributed to Frederick the Great who employed a number of galloper guns firing 3-pound shot. Their

Galloper gun

success led the British to use an even lighter version firing 1½-pound shot which was often drawn by two horses to achieve greater mobility.

The practice of mounting several gun barrels on one carriage to fire a kind of broadside had been tried out since the earliest days of artillery. Both the French and German armies were using triple-barrelled cannon as field guns early in the eighteenth century. This same idea had been tried out with batteries of musket barrels or miniature cannon mounted on a cart or wooden barricade that could be dragged into place to strengthen a defensive position or cover a road. These battery weapons often incorporated an elementary breech-loading mechanism, as at close range the gunners could hardly run out in front of the barricade to re-load the multiple barrels.

PUCKLE'S GUN

One invention of this period stands out. It was a machine gun patented in 1718 by James Puckle, an English inventor who was by profession a Notary Public or solicitor. Puckle was a man of strong views who had published a book on the evils of drinking, and the prototype of his gun is engraved with the exhortation, 'defending King George, your country and laws is

Puckle's machine gun

defending yourselves and Protestant cause'. Puckle's machine gun was made of brass and mounted on a very modern-looking tripod with a 'crane to rise, fall and turn the gun round'. A cylinder with six to nine chambers held the cartridges. A turn of the cylinder brought a cartridge opposite the open breech and a half turn of the crank handle closed the chamber on to the rear end of the barrel. Each chamber had to be primed through a small touch hole, and the gun was fired by a conventional flint-lock mechanism fitted to the barrel. The weakness of this design was the loose-fitting breech mechanism which allowed a lot of gas to escape. Nevertheless, the *London Journal* reported a demonstration carried out in 1722 when sixty-three rounds were fired in seven minutes in wet weather, which was a remarkable achievement. Presumably, the operator had a number of cylinders already loaded and an assistant to help in changing them. Nothing is known of the range or penetrating power of this invention which is the only machine gun attributed to an English inventor. It never went into production and it appears to have been forgotten for over a hundred years. A somewhat similar idea was developed by a Swiss inventor in 1742. A small copper cannon was adapted by cutting a slot at the touch-hole end of the barrel. A panel holding ten cartridges was pushed through this slot so that each charge could be fired in turn. It is likely that this invention failed for the same reason as Puckle's: too much gas escaped, and there was a danger of premature explosion.

JOHN CHURCHILL

Although the eighteenth century saw the birth of many inventions that later revolutionised industry, in the realms of military technology there were no dramatic changes. Because of the expense of maintaining a standing army the tendency was to make do with the weapons already to hand. As all European armies were armed and equipped very much alike, generalship was the key to success. New tactics began to emerge and these, together with the problems of training and of what we now call 'man management', had to be closely studied by any commander who sought to outwit, outmarch and outfight his adversary. Such a general was John Churchill, first Duke of Marlborough, one of the greatest commanders of his or any age. John Churchill, the illustrious ancestor of Sir Winston Churchill, had joined the King's Regiment of Foot Guards in 1667 at the age of seventeen. Seven years later he was in command of the regiment, having served with distinction under Marshal Turenne. When the War of the Spanish Succession broke out in 1702 Queen Anne turned to him to take command of the army as Captain General. Marlborough expected a lot of his men and worked them hard. He proved a strict disciplinarian, especially as regards behaviour in a foreign country, but he also took every care for the well-being of the soldiers who were well fed and regularly paid. His great personal charm and extreme

3-pounder regimental gun

coolness and gallantry in action made him loved as few generals have been, and throughout the army he was affectionately known as Corporal John. Marlborough certainly earned the respect of his country's enemies, and Voltaire described him as, 'more of a King than William III, as much of a statesman, and a far greater captain'. He had a flair for not only misleading his adversary, but for delivering his main attack at the weak spot with the utmost vigour. To achieve this he trained his army to manœuvre and fight so that each arm supported the other. Guns were placed to support the infantry, and the infantry was placed to support the cavalry. No practical detail escaped Marlborough's eye, and he would put the whole army through its exercises, using a flag and beat of drum to control each manœuvre, until every man knew the part he must play. When the French cavalry adopted pistol-proof cuirasses, Marlborough ordered each member of his own cavalry to be issued with a single breastplate, but he only allowed each trooper three charges of powder and ball for a whole campaign, and these could only be used when guarding the horses at grass. Unlike the French, who mixed infantry with the cavalry, who were still trained to rely on their carbines, Marlborough's squadrons charged with the sword alone and a reserve was always held back to be launched at the decisive moment. Marlborough employed his cavalry in heavy masses. Enormous lines of charging horsemen poured over a whole section of the battlefield, and many of his victories were won in this way. In the setting up of these sweeping cavalry charges the other arms played a vital part. Marlborough paid great attention to his artillery, and at the Battle of Blenheim in 1704 each gun was laid under his own eye. Similarly, the fire discipline and steadiness of his infantry was so excellent that counter-attacks could be beaten off by volley fire alone, and only the front rank was required to re-load with fixed bayonets.

British cavalry trooper at the time of the Battle of Blenheim

53

The importance of co-operation between arms is illustrated by two battles fought in Scotland after the Jacobite rebellion of 1745. At Falkirk in 1746, the English formed up without waiting for their guns. The battle opened with an abortive charge by the dragoons against the unbroken front of the Jacobites. Then the front rank of Highlanders, who had opened fire at about sixty paces, threw down their muskets and, armed with sword and targe, fell on the left flank of the English infantry and drove them from the field in disorder. Only the steadiness of three regiments on the right flank prevented a complete defeat. Three months later, at the Battle of Culloden, the English guns succeeded in goading the Highlanders into making a similar charge which at first had some success, but was successfully repelled by the second line of English infantry. A charge by the English dragoons settled the matter and the battle was over in half an hour. The orders to the English infantry are of interest; each man was to hold his fire until the Highlanders were within ten paces and then to use his bayonet to thrust, not at his own assailant who could parry with his targe, but at the Highlander attacking the man on his right hand.

CHARLES XII OF SWEDEN

The revival of the cavalry arm owed much to the impetuous and fiery Charles XII, King of Sweden from 1697–1718. A man of extraordinary energy who delighted in hand-to-hand combat, he trained his cavalry to manœuvre at speed and charge with the sword alone. To achieve maximum speed and endurance his cavalry wore no armour and were forbidden to use any kind of firearm. The sword was long and straight, and used principally for thrusting. Similarly, the Swedish infantry were practised in bayonet charges and rarely executed the slow, methodical movements employed in other European armies. Charles XII relied on his cavalry to follow him over the most difficult country and charge any kind of opposition, even entrenched positions. His tenacity and dash were by-words, and on one occasion he followed up a retreating Saxon force of 10,000 men of all arms for nine consecutive days without unsaddling. Catching up with the Saxons near their own frontier he routed their cavalry with the only two regiments that had kept up with him and then turned back to attack the remainder of the force, capturing all the guns and driving the Saxon infantry, who only escaped under cover of darkness, across the frontier.

In 1709, at the Battle of Pultowa, Charles XII was decisively defeated by Peter the Great of Russia. The Czar, who knew the quality of his troops in defence, had taken up a position based on a series of redoubts that each contained guns and two battalions of infantry. Large gaps separated the redoubts and through these gaps bodies of Russian infantry and cavalry, working in close co-operation, launched strong counter-attacks. The Swedish troops fought with great bravery but their attacks never broke through the chain of redoubts and, although they re-formed and fought on for some hours, the co-ordinated attacks of the Russians decided the day.

PETER THE GREAT OF RUSSIA

When Peter the Great came to the throne in 1682 his army consisted of two dragoon regiments and twenty-seven infantry regiments, but within ten years he had increased his cavalry force to thirty-three regiments of dragoons, including three of dragoon grenadiers. The Russian dragoons were armed with muskets, pistols and a long, straight sword, and nearly half of them carried either an axe, a spade or a large shovel attached to the saddle. Their uniform was a blue coat, a waistcoat and trousers made of chamois leather, spurred boots

55

Russian dragoon 1700–20

and the usual three-cornered hat. Ensigns and non-commissioned officers were armed only with a sword and pistol.

Although the dragoons formed the main part of the regular cavalry, in the Russian Army they were extensively used in an infantry role, and at one period they were issued with sword bayonets which were later replaced by the type of socket bayonet normally issued to the infantry. At about this time Peter the Great raised several hussar regiments, recruited from Hungary and Serbia, to increase his regular cavalry. He also organised a Horse regiment for his personal protection (called Life Guards), which consisted entirely of noblemen who were under training to become cavalry officers. The cost of maintaining the foreign hussar regiments, however, proved very expensive and most of Peter the Great's light cavalry were irregulars. These were the famous Cossacks who were usually employed on outpost duties and for skirmishing and attacking convoys, leaving the dragoons free to act as shock troops in co-operation with the remainder of the regular forces. Under Peter the Great the Russian Army gained a great reputation for steadiness in action and always fought with great bravery and tenacity when repelling an attack or in the defence of fortifications.

MAURICE DE SAXE

Maurice de Saxe, Marshal of France during the War of the Austrian Succession, 1740–48, restored to the French Army much of the prestige they had lost at the hands of Marlborough. As a General he was a flamboyant yet paternal figure who inspired his troops to fight for the glory of France, but shared their hardships and was always concerned for their welfare. He was also the most prominent military theorist and writer of his times. His famous book, *Mes Rêveries*, which described the organisation of the perfect army, was only published after his death and many of his ideas were never tried out, as the military successes of Frederick the Great had meanwhile led to the adoption of Prussian doctrine and manuals.

A Cossack

De Saxe employed heavy cavalry as shock troops, and together with the heavy artillery they were always kept with the main army. The heavy horsemen, who were called Uhlans, wore a cuirass and helmet and were armed with a breech-loading carbine (which de Saxe himself had invented) slung on a bandolier and a 4-foot sword, but carried no pistols. The front rank carried 12-foot lances which weighed six pounds and were also used for tent poles. The majority of the cavalry, however, were dragoons who were lightly equipped and mounted on small, active horses. De Saxe insisted on his cavalry being trained to keep good order when charging at the gallop, and said that any squadron that could not charge 2,000 paces at full speed without breaking was not fit for active service. The dragoons were not only used for reconnoitring and outpost duty,

57

but were also trained to skirmish in front of the army. The third rank was specially drilled to work in open order and then retire rapidly and form up in the rear. As de Saxe placed such importance on mobility and offensive action it is strange to read in his book that he considered dragoons should all carry lances which could be used as pikes when dismounted, and that all cavalry should wear light armour.

De Saxe trained his infantry to march in step, a practice that was soon copied by other countries. If he had had his way his soldiers would also have given up the elaborate military coiffure then in vogue and the infantry would have worn light helmets, loose-fitting doublets, and supple, tallow-greased shoes, with wooden overshoes to wear in the winter. De Saxe, who was German by birth, well understood the temperament of the French soldiers, describing them as 'brave to excess but unstable'. Consequently, he used mixed tactical formations of all arms, made up if possible of small units of hardened regulars. In defence, he made use of every natural advantage of the terrain and he employed large numbers of pioneers (foot soldiers trained and equipped to build roads, bridges and field works) to build redoubts, which were carefully sited to give enfilade fire. The redoubts were usually square wooden blockades of felled tree trunks, each with a self-contained infantry garrison and guns sited to fire into the flanks of advancing infantry, de Saxe's idea being to draw his opponent onto ground of his own choice where the counter-blow could be delivered. Such tactics were a complete breakaway from the conventional linear battle formations.

At the battle of Fontenoy in 1745, the French left flank was protected by a wood and two redoubts. The little hamlet of Fontenoy was fortified and supported by three more redoubts thrown back at a right angle towards the River Scheldt. The open ground near the river was only held by dragoons and hussars, an unusual

Austrian hussar

and daring expedient. De Saxe then placed his main
force and reserves to cover the vital central sector of
less than half a mile between the wood and Fontenoy,
but he sent a further but smaller reserve force of all
arms, with twelve out of his sixty guns, right back to
watch the bridges over the river and cover his left flank.
The inexperienced Duke of Cumberland decided to
make the main Allied attack against the centre of the
position using the British and some Hanoverian infantry. Led by the Brigade of Guards and on a front
of only three battalions, this force of twenty battalions
in an almost solid formation penetrated 300 yards into
the French lines. The square had marched forward
with awe-inspiring steadiness, the men stepping short
so that platoons in turn could step out, halt and fire.
There was no room to deploy or pass through the
cavalry, and the Allied infantry were caught in a heavy
cross fire. Charged in front and on their flank by the
French dragoons they were slowly forced back. On

59

British grenadier

their left the Austrian and Dutch assault on Fontenoy
and the three redoubts also failed. A second attack in
the centre was ordered but met a similar fate, although
the British battalions penetrated so far into the French
camp that the guns in the redoubts were firing into
their rear. Calling up his last reserves, de Saxe finally
succeeded in repulsing the attack, but the British and

French infantry 1745

Hanoverian infantry had suffered 6,000 casualties, one-third of their strength. At last Cumberland gave the order to retreat, and the depleted battalions fell back without confusion or wavering, covered by rear guards that halted in turn every hundred paces to fire a volley. As the two armies slowly disengaged, the British cavalry charged again and again to check the pursuit, but the French had had enough. Fontenoy, the French victory that so nearly was a defeat, was de Saxe's greatest achievement, but it also demonstrated to the whole of Europe the quality of the British infantry.

FREDERICK THE GREAT

Frederick II, King of Prussia from 1740–86, known as Frederick the Great, inherited an army of 83,000 men. In return for the peasants on their estates being reduced to serfdom, the nobles or 'Junkers' gave the King absolute power and helped finance the army. Part of

61

the agreement was that the *élite* officer corps, which enjoyed many privileges, should be recruited from the 'Junker' class. In the Prussian military academies the cadets were given a practical military education and were not only subjected to rigorous discipline, but inculcated with a high sense of patriotism. The soldiers were chosen from a roll of all males in each canton and engagement was practically for life. After training they were sent home, but called up for two to three months each year. Half the men were foreigners who had enlisted for the bounty. Frederick had a passion for tall men and spent nearly two million pounds on recruiting a regiment of giant grenadiers, many of whom had been literally kidnapped and forced to enlist. Frederick insisted that the men should learn to fear their officers more than the enemy, but he also did a great deal to foster an *esprit de corps*. Every regiment had distinctive trimmings on their uniform and the men were taught to believe their own regiment to be the best in the army. Because the soldiers deserted whenever possible, individual initiative was discouraged, falling out on the line of march was absolutely forbidden and loose fighting or skirmishing was avoided. Even encampments in the field were enclosed with trenches or breast works and patrolled. All training indeed aimed at mechanical precision and absolute rigidity enforced by severe discipline. The infantry formed in three ranks with the men shoulder to shoulder. With the files touching (only one foot, nine inches was allowed for each man), uniforms had to be modified and became tight-fitting and uncomfortable. For the same reason the cartridge case, haversack and sword were slung farther back from cross belts. All three ranks loaded and fired with fixed bayonets. Volleys were fired by odd- and even-numbered platoons in sequence. Each man carried thirty cartridges and was trained to fire five rounds a minute. Endless marching and drilling in close order enabled the Prussian battalions to form line or square from column quicker

Prussian grenadier in Frederick the Great's army

than their opponents and immediately advance to the attack, still in perfect order.

It was, however, with his cavalry that Frederick the Great won most of his battles. When he came to the throne he found the regiments incapable of rapid manœuvre, being only trained to fight in line and rely on their carbines, whether mounted or on foot. All this was quickly changed. The equipment was lightened and the use of firearms by mounted troops was forbidden. Offensive action with the sword alone became the rule and the officers were always to be the first to charge. Frederick insisted that before a soldier was admitted to his regiment he must be thoroughly grounded in horsemanship and the use of the sword. This training in the riding schools proved to be the key to manœuvring at speed. Squadrons were drilled to keep their alignment over long distances. With careful training, mass

Prussian cuirassier

lines of 8,000 to 10,000 horsemen charging knee to knee over hundreds of yards could be halted and immediately launched in a fresh direction, all in perfect line. In practising these mass manœuvres men were often killed when charging over broken ground. The Prussian cavalry contained cuirassiers, dragoons and hussars, but they were all trained alike and were completely interchangeable as regards carrying out such duties as reconnaissance, searching woods, guarding defiles, patrolling or finding outposts. Having to operate in small parties and even individually meant the men had to be completely trustworthy, and they were chosen with great care from among the sons of small landowners or farmers. If a trooper deserted the parents were held responsible for both man and horse.

As already mentioned, Frederick employed his cavalry in battle in large masses and realised that this made them vulnerable to the deadly effects of gun and volley fire. This led to his introduction of horse artillery which could keep up with the cavalry and pave the way for the massed charge. The guns were 6-pounders, and the whole gun detachment was mounted. One of

Battle of Leuthen

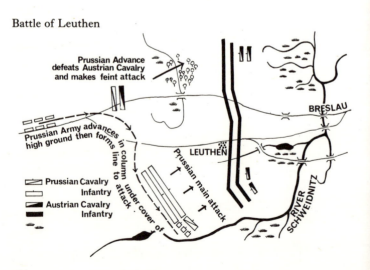

Frederick's favourite tactical manœuvres, which was slavishly imitated by many of his opponents, is often referred to as the oblique order of attack. This was a manœuvre which enabled the main attack to be launched with a superior force against one flank of the enemy's line. The superior discipline and training in close-order drill of the Prussian troops made this possible over open ground, but ideally Frederick always tried to disguise his intentions by using darkness or dead ground (where his troops would be hidden from the enemy) to cover the advance of his main force while a feint attack kept his enemy occupied. At the battle of Leuthen in 1757, where he was outnumbered by the Austrians (under Prince Charles of Lorraine) by two to one, Frederick won his greatest tactical victory in this manner. The Austrians with about 60,000 men held a somewhat extended front of over five miles, with a stream to their rear and both flanks resting on marshy ground. As dawn broke the Prussian advance guard succeeded in driving in the cavalry outposts and Frederick ordered this success to be followed up immediately by a feint attack against the Austrian right flank, but only using the advance guard that was already deployed. Believing this to be the start of the main assault the Austrians reinforced their right flank, but all this time Frederick's main force had been marching across the front, keeping below the crest of some high ground, to attack the southern flank of the Austrian positions. The subsequent battle was long and bloody, but the Austrians never recovered from their initial mistake of moving their reserves too soon. Outmanœuvred as well as deceived, the Austrians were unable to withstand the concentrated attacks which finally enveloped and rolled up their left flank. The Prussian casualties were heavy— 6,400 killed and wounded, but the Austrians suffered a complete defeat and the loss of a third of their army.

Chapter Four

Lessons from the New World

IMPROVEMENTS IN ARTILLERY

In the second half of the eighteenth century significant improvements in the manufacture of artillery pieces took place. Through the discovery of coke smelting, better and cheaper iron guns could be manufactured, and a new method of drilling out the bore made for stronger barrels and greater accuracy. Through his invention of the 'ballistic pendulum' Benjamin Robins was able to measure the effectiveness of a charge of powder in relation to gun barrels of different length and weight. He proved that guns could be made shorter

Ballistic pendulum

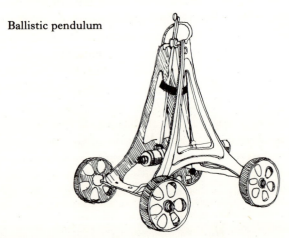

and lighter without loss of range. In France, at about the same time as Robins' theories were published, General Vaquette de Gribeauval was appointed Inspector General of the French Artillery, and proceeded to introduce numerous reforms, all aimed at making the French Artillery more efficient and mobile. Regimental guns were standardised as 4-pounders, while the larger 8- and 12-pounders and 6-inch mortars were organised in batteries as a reserve. Twelve- and sixteen-pounders and mortars up to twelve inches became standard fortress artillery. All gun carriages for use in the field were made to a uniform pattern with interchangeable parts, and were drawn by horses harnessed in pairs. Limber boxes were fitted to the regimental guns and the whole emphasis was on mobility so that both these light field guns and the reserve batteries could keep up on the line of march and deploy quickly. A British introduction of the same period was the block trail

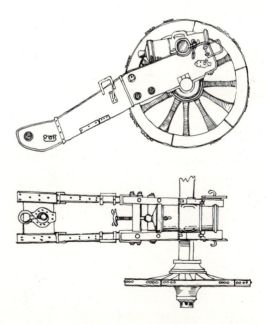

6-inch howitzer on Gribeauval's standard gun carriage

Royal Horse Artillery

which was first used for 3-pounder infantry guns, and for the 6-pounders of the Royal Horse Artillery, which was raised by the Duke of Richmond in 1792.

As guns became more mobile so more and more artillery was used in battle and ammunition columns grew longer and longer. The protection of the batteries and their supply columns soon required special mobile troops and contributed to the formation of light-infantry regiments and the increased use of light cavalry.

SHOT AND SHELL

Grape-shot

In addition to the conventional solid shot, guns also fired case-shot or grape-shot. Both of the latter were for use against troops in the open. Case-shot consisted of a flimsy canister filled with musket balls. The canister often failed to break up in flight and the effective range of case-shot was only about 300 yards. Grape-shot had a wood or metal base with a pillar to which iron balls were tied by cords and held in place by a cloth cover. When the round of grape-shot was fired the explosion of the charge ignited the cloth and cord and the balls were released, towards the end of their flight, in the form of a spray of flying bullets. The range, like that of case-shot, was very short.

During the Great Siege of Gibraltar, in 1779, part of the Spanish lines were along high sand banks over 2,000 yards from the fortress guns. Solid shot merely plunged into the sand, and at this extreme range the 'Royal' mortars were inaccurate, and many of the mortar

68

shells (still shaped like, but no longer called, bombs) were smothered in the sand. An infantry officer, a certain Captain John Mercer of the 39th Regiment of Foot, made the novel suggestion of firing 5·5-inch mortar shells from 24-pounder guns (which were of the correct calibre) but using short fuses on the shells so that they would explode in the air above the sand dunes. Although reasonably successful in harassing the Spanish working parties, these shells caused few casualties as they only broke into a small number of large pieces. The real solution was found by Lieutenant Henry Shrapnel of the Royal Artillery in 1784, but his invention was ignored for twenty years. Shrapnel's 'spherical case' was a hollow shell fitted with a fuse and containing a number of round shot and a small charge of powder. The fuse was made of wood with a core of powder and the outside was 'ribbed' so that it could be cut off to burn for an exact fraction of time. The fuse was calculated to ignite the charge above the target, the charge being only just sufficient to open the shell. The small shot then continued in their original line of flight at a slightly increased velocity. Shrapnel shells made. on this principle were used in many armies for over a century, right up to the end of the Great War.

THE KENTUCKY RIFLE

Since the beginning of the eighteenth century rifles had been manufactured in America in increasing numbers by German gunsmiths who had settled in Pennsylvania. Originally, these were large-bore hunting rifles similar to those used in Europe but they proved far too heavy to be carried for weeks on end by frontiersmen trekking through virgin forests and over great mountain ranges. A large-bore rifle with perhaps six months' supply of powder and shot, together with ramrod and hammer, might well weigh as much as seventy or eighty pounds. What was needed, both for

Kentucky rifle

shooting game or as a defence against marauding Indians, was a much lighter rifle which was easy to load, reliable and accurate. Sheer necessity drove the gunsmiths to endless experiment. The calibre of barrels was reduced from ·75 to as small as ·55 or ·40 inch, allowing the weight of bullet to be reduced to thirty-six or even seventy-three to a pound. Very slender stocks of maple wood were used and the barrels were lengthened (to about 42–48 inches) so as to increase the muzzle velocity. The use of the hammer was abandoned. Easy loading as well as a tight fit was achieved by placing a small patch of greased leather over the bore before the ball was rammed home, which could be done with easy strokes. It was quickly found that this technique avoided distortion of the bullet and damage to the rifling and that the greased patch made such an effective gas check that high velocities were achieved with relatively small charges. The result was a very flat trajectory up to at least 150 yards and increased accuracy at longer ranges.

These rifles became known as Kentucky rifles, a name that probably originated from a ballad about the exploits of men from Kentucky in the Battle of New Orleans in 1815, and the name has been used ever since. The maple-wood stocks had a very distinctive crescent shape, and a little box, usually fitted with a brass lid, was let into the right side of the stock to take the grease patches. These rifles, designed to meet the exacting requirements of the American frontiersmen, were destined to play an increasing part in the fighting that broke out in America between the French and the British and later in the War of Independence.

THE FERGUSON RIFLE

When Captain Patrick Ferguson, a thirty-two-year-old officer of the 71st Highlanders, patented his new rifle, he had been on active service since the age of fifteen and was the finest shot in the British Army. The rifle

70

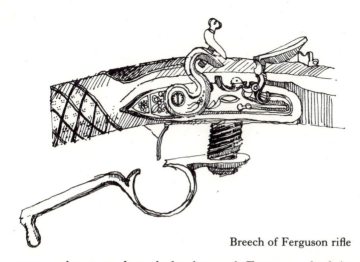

Breech of Ferguson rifle

was a plug-type breech loader and Ferguson had in
fact struck on the essential modifications to a design
made fifty years before by a Huguenot refugee. A hole
was drilled vertically right through the rear end of the
breech to take a specially designed screw plug. The
base of the plug was attached to the front of the trigger
guard, one half turn of which closed the breech, or
conversely withdrew the plug sufficiently to allow a
ball and charge to be loaded through the open hole on
the top of the breech. The breech chamber was wider
than the rest of the bore so that the ball ran forward a
little way to leave room for the charge to be poured in.
Earlier attempts to use screw plugs had proved un-
satisfactory because they jammed through fouling.
Ferguson found an effective solution by cutting channels
in the plug to keep it free. The Ferguson rifle had a
number of very practical advantages: the plug could
not fall out and was virtually gas-tight; loading through
the hole on the top of the rifle was simple and quick
and, as was not true for a muzzle loader, could be done
while the marksman was lying down or even running
forward. Although the ball fitted loosely in the chamber
it was exactly the size of the bore so that the initial
resistance was greater when it was forced into the
rifling and it left the muzzle with increased spin. At a

71

Egg's carbine

demonstration at Woolwich Ferguson created quite a sensation with his new rifle. According to a report in the *Annual Register* he kept up a steady fire in pouring rain of four to six rounds a minute, firing at 200 yards with remarkable accuracy. To the astonishment of a number of senior officers he then showed that he could still fire four accurate shots a minute while lying on his back or even running forward over rough ground. Only about 200 Ferguson rifles were manufactured. These were of ·68-inch calibre with short barrels, 34–36 inches long, and rifled with eight grooves. As far as range and accuracy were concerned, the rifle was the best in the world and it was so much easier to load, that trained soldiers could fire as fast as eight rounds a minute. Many people now think that if Ferguson's rifle had been generally adopted in the British Army the course of the American War of Independence* might well have been dramatically changed. Ferguson was given command of 100 men who were equipped with his rifle and sent to America to serve under Lieutenant General William Howe. On arrival, they were issued with green uniforms and played an important role at the Battle of Brandywine, in which Ferguson was wounded and subsequently lost the use of one arm. His company was broken up and the rifles put into store. Ferguson himself was killed a few years later in the Battle of King's Mountain and only one of the rifles has since been found. The lack of official interest in this remarkable rifle may have been because it did not fire the standard service cartridge, but it is more likely because it was thought to be too accurate. Some senior officers took the view that few British soldiers could judge distances as the American frontiersmen could do and so would gain no advantage from a more accurate rifle, while back in Britain the Generals still thought in terms of the Brown Bess and short-range volley fire.

* Better known in America as the American Revolution.

The Duke of Richmond who was Master General of Ordnance, however, could see the merit in a breech-loading mechanism for cavalry carbines and also for the ordinary musket so that the infantry could fire a greater number of volleys. In 1788 a certain Durs Egg, copying a design which was already in use in the Austrian Army, produced a carbine with a tip-up chamber to take the standard cartridge. Before firing, the chamber was locked in position by a lever which engaged two claws on the top of the barrel. Egg's carbine, which had a rifled barrel, two feet, four inches long, was fitted with a long, thin bayonet which looked exactly like a spear. A rather similar design for a breech-loading musket had been made in 1786 by Henry Nock, whose workshop was in Ludgate Hill, but like Egg's carbine it was never manufactured in quantity. Nock became quite famous for his seven-barrelled volley gun which was supplied to the Royal Navy, and also for a very powerful double-barrelled pistol with a detachable butt that could be fired from the shoulder which he made for the Royal Horse Artillery. With the outbreak of the Napoleonic Wars in 1803 there was no time for further experiments and the cheap, and easily manufactured, muzzle loaders were issued just as fast as they could be produced.

British light dragoon

LIGHT INFANTRY

Although Prussian doctrine still dominated the Continental armies a military revolution was about to take place, just as a social revolution was about to break out in France and spread to many parts of Europe. More and more light cavalry and infantry were now used, not only for guarding convoys, but also for outpost duty and for providing a screen of skirmishers to cover the manœuvring of the main army. These light troops were either raised as independent companies, known as 'free corps', like the Polish mounted scouts employed by the

French and the Jaeger riflemen used by the Prussians, or were recruited from amongst smugglers and vagabonds who knew the country well. The practice of employing grenadiers for detached duties and skirmishing was gradually dropped and light companies of small and active men now formed part of the regimental organisation. These light companies, like the grenadier companies, were sometimes brought together to form special battalions. In the French Army several complete battalions of *chasseurs-à-pied* were raised in about 1780. The difference between such light troops and the normal infantry of the line was not so much in their

Chasseur à pied

arms and equipment as in their role as skirmishers and protective troops. In the British Army the evolution of light infantry came as a direct result of the fighting in America. Here new tactical doctrines were being learned the hard way. In the closely wooded and mountainous country, parade ground drill movements became meaningless and the new disciplines of field craft and marksmanship demanded a fresh approach to training methods and leadership. Fortunately some of the younger regimental officers and brigadiers were quick to adapt themselves to the new conditions of warfare. Unfortunately many of the older commanders were quite unable to see the need for change.

BRADDOCK AT THE MONONGAHELA

In North America, the French were determined to seize control of the waterways that linked the Saint Lawrence to the Gulf of Mexico and thus prevent the British colonists from expanding westwards. In 1755, the British decided to capture the French Fort Duquesne on the Ohio, and General Edward Braddock was dispatched with a mixed force of British infantry and Virginia militiamen on the long march through a wilderness of forest and mountain. General Braddock, 'a martinet of the worst type, but brave as a lion', with forty-five years' experience of European warfare, believed that war could only be fought by the drill manual. He also insisted on taking an enormous baggage train and 600 pack animals through country where there was virtually no fodder. A third of his force fell sick and had to be left in a base camp and under conditions of great hardship the remainder, some 1,450 men with ten field guns and a number of pack animals, eventually reached a point on the River Monongahela only a few miles from the fort. Meanwhile, the French Commander had reinforced his small garrison of regular infantry with a number of Canadians and Indians whose scouts had reported Braddock's advance day by day. The French now planned to ambush the British column at a ford over the river and a company of regulars with some Canadians and over 600 Indians set off under Captain Beaujoy, but by the time the Indians were assembled Braddock's force had already crossed the ford. Ahead, a narrow path led across a wide and bushy ravine overlooked by a hill. The advance was led by a strong advance guard and 300 axe men who were needed to clear a road for the guns and baggage trains. The remaining troops marched in the forest on either side of the baggage column. The order of march had been suggested by one of Braddock's staff, Lieutenant Colonel George Washington of the Virginia militia, and confirmed at a Council of War. Unfortunately practically all of the fifty Indian scouts, who had been recruited for the expedition, had tired of the delays and in particular of their treatment and had returned to their homes. One chief later complained that Braddock 'looked upon us as dogs, and would never hear anything that we said to him'. Braddock had done all he knew to guard against surprise but it was not enough. Had he known how to handle the Indian scouts the disaster that followed might have been avoided. Suddenly, just when the advance guard had crossed the ravine, a man in Indian dress, Captain Beaujoy himself, stepped into their path and gave a signal. In a moment a war cry was echoing through the forest and a deadly fire poured into the ranks of the redcoats who had now formed line. The British volleys crashed out but not an enemy was in sight. Now the main body pressed forward, spurred on by Braddock who arrived to find a scene of utter confusion. The remnants of the advance guard were slowly falling back, having abandoned their guns, and as more and more companies rushed forward they came under a withering fire seemingly coming from all

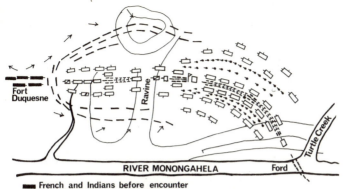

French and Indians before encounter
--- Encircling positions during battle
BRITISH ▭-cavalry patrol ▭-infantry ≡field gun ⊐ wagons and carts
←cattle and packhorses ▭ flank guard

Braddock's defeat

directions. Those who tried to shoot back from the cover of trees were beaten into line by Braddock with the flat of his sword. For three hours the ranks held. Men fell where they stood, never having seen their opponents hidden in the forest. Braddock, who had had four horses shot under him, finally ordered a withdrawal and the remnants of his force poured back over the ford in an almost uncontrollable rout. The defeat was crushing. The British casualties amounted to nearly a thousand officers and men. The total French loss was fifteen, and their Indian allies lost less than fifty killed and wounded. Braddock was carried from the field mortally wounded and his dying words were, 'we shall better know how to deal with them another time'. Braddock's disastrous defeat brought no dramatic changes to the drill manuals, however. The training of the regular and provincial troops still started and ended on the parade ground. Many senior officers were quite unable to grasp that conditions in America were utterly different from anything they had met in Europe. The lead had to come from a handful of younger men.

ROGERS' RANGERS

Robert Rogers, born in a frontier village in New Hampshire, was one of the first to show what could

One of Rogers' Rangers

be done by resolute men who were prepared to emulate
the Indians' stealth and cunning. Rogers had for years
been engaged in the smuggling trade with Canada. To
trek for weeks, confident in his skill as a woodsman to
pass undetected through the wildest country, was no
new experience for Rogers and the men he recruited
into his famous companies of Rangers. The Rangers
wore the practical clothes of the frontiersmen, only
relying on some distinctive mark to distinguish each
company. Their weapons were the smooth-bore gun
loaded with buckshot, bullets or sometimes both, and
the woodsman's axe and hunting knife that they
habitually carried. Some of Rogers' best-known exploits took place around Lakes George and Champlain
and the French-held forts of Crown Point and Ticonderoga. Across the lakes in flimsy canoes and through
the forests, parties of Rangers moved by day and
night, winter and summer, almost at will, and this in
spite of the Indians who were set to search the area
and the fortified camps and outposts that guarded the

approaches to the forts. Setting ambushes, capturing supply wagons, terrorising the outlying settlements and attacking the French outposts, Rogers and his men continually kept the French commanders guessing as to where he would strike next. On one occasion in deep winter, Rogers with about seventy men was operating only three miles from Fort Ticonderoga when he learned from prisoners that the French had assembled over 600 troops and a number of Indians to cut all communications back to the British forts on which he was based. On their return march the Rangers beat off a determined attack by over 200 French troops supported by a number of Indians. The fighting lasted for several hours, and Rogers displayed great skill in preventing his position from being over-run from the rear. The Rangers lost fourteen killed and six men made prisoner before Rogers successfully withdrew his force under cover of darkness. The French claimed they had only lost forty men, but their casualties must have been considerably greater, as the French commander at Fort Ticonderoga immediately sent for large reinforcements.

Some of the British officers serving in America had already realised the importance of learning the new kind of warfare practised by Rogers and his Rangers. One of these, Brigadier Lord George Augustus Howe, a young nobleman in his early thirties who was commanding a battalion of British infantry, spent many months studying the art of forest warfare. He accompanied Rogers on his scouting expeditions, sharing the hardships and self-imposed discipline of the Rangers. Soon Lord Howe was introducing reforms into his own regiment. Officers and men alike were made to wear their hair cut close, and to cut off the tails of their uniform coats and wear leggings. No one was allowed to carry more than one blanket and an officer's baggage was reduced to a small portmanteau. Equipment was cut to a minimum and every man had to carry thirty pounds of meal in his knapsack, so that the whole battalion would not need supplies for a month. Finally, the musket barrels were browned so they would not catch the light, and the men were practised in scouting and woodcraft. Officers accustomed to all the usual comforts of camp life, with many servants and camp followers to carry their baggage, wait on them and wash their linen, quickly learned that Lord Howe practised what he preached. Having been invited to dine in his tent, they found themselves seated on logs, with a bearskin for a carpet. A servant now appeared with some wooden platters and a large dish of pork and peas which was placed on the ground. Taking from his pocket a wooden sheath containing a knife and fork his Lordship now began to eat his meal. The guests could only look on in embarrassment until Lord Howe, remarking that they must have come on the campaign without providing themselves with what was necessary, handed each one a sheath with a knife and fork like his own.

THE HEIGHTS OF ABRAHAM

Lord Howe was killed during an attack on Fort Ticonderoga, but his brother, William Howe, who was a major at the time, led the light infantry assault up the 200-foot cliffs of the Saint Lawrence River to reach the heights of Abraham above Quebec. The battle that followed resulted in the total defeat of the French under Field Marshal Louis Joseph de Montcalm and the conquest of Canada. This feat of arms showed what could be achieved by well-trained infantry in co-operation with the Royal Navy. The British commander, Major General James Wolfe, successfully landed about 3,500 men by night on the banks of the Saint Lawrence at a point so inaccessible that the French had hardly bothered to guard the precipitous path up from the beach. By daybreak on 13th September, 1759, Wolfe had assembled his whole force on the plain which over-looked the city. Montcalm was completely deceived as to the place of landing, and had to force-march his troops from the other side of Quebec. The French infantry and Canadian militia totalled some 4,500 men and as soon as they were assembled Montcalm launched his attack. The thin line of British infantry standing three deep made no move until the French attack was almost on them. Then the order rang out for volley fire by platoons. With the British ranks stepping forward with perfect discipline to clear the smoke and at a range of less than thirty paces, a general volley crashed into the French ranks. The action lasted only a few minutes, and as the British rushed forward with bayonet and claymore the French broke and poured back towards the city in utter confusion.

Wolfe's death on the battlefield was a grave loss to his country. He had been one of the first of a new breed of British Army officer, a humanitarian as well as a disciplinarian; a General who could use a rifle better than most of the marksmen in his army, and who insisted that his officers follow his example by carrying a rifle in action. Wolfe was one of the first British commanders to organise and train special light infantry units made up of picked marksmen from the line regiments.

THE ROYAL AMERICANS

A regiment that fought with distinction under Wolfe was the Royal Americans which later became the 60th, King's Royal Rifle Corps. Several battalions were raised in 1756, having been recruited from the western part of Pennsylvania where there was a mixed population of English, Swiss and German settlers. Two very experienced young Swiss-born officers, who had fought under the French in Europe—Colonels Henri Bouquet and Frederick Haldimand—were appointed the first

Private, Royal
Americans

battalion commanders. The Royal Americans were
originally issued with regulation red tunics but soon
appeared in less obvious uniforms. Some units wore
blue and some 'a green jacket and drawers with ruffs
of bearskin round the neck'. They were armed with
a fusil, cartridge box and powder horn and the officers
received a special issue of rifled carbines. Like George
Washington, Bouquet was always agitating to dress his
men like Indians and his training methods were quite
revolutionary. Cleanliness and a soldier-like manner
came first, then the men were taught to walk properly,
to run in ranks in extended order and to disperse and
rally at given signals, also 'to leap logs and ditches and

82

carry burdens proportionate to their strength'. Only then was the recruit given his rifle, taught marksmanship and practised all over again in the various exercises he had been previously given. The men were taught to swim rivers, 'pushing before them on a small raft their clothes, arms and ammunition', to use snowshoes, build canoes and construct almost everything they needed from an oven to a cart, as well as bridges and log cabins, from the timber and other materials taken from the forest. Parties of men under an officer were sent out on hunting expeditions for weeks on end, taking only a little flour and having to live on the game they shot and the fish they could catch. The Royal Americans soon became not only good carpenters, masons, tailors and shoemakers, but admirable soldiers trained in a new kind of team spirit. Every officer or man on discharge received a grant of land according to rank: 5,000 acres for a field officer, down to 200 acres for a private.

In 1763, only eight years after Braddock's humiliating defeat, the Royal Americans played a major role in the expedition led by Colonel Bouquet against the Indians in what was known as the French and Indian War. Bouquet's tactical doctrine is of interest. Having argued that Indian tactics were to surround their enemy, to fight in a scattered formation, and never to stand their ground when attacked, but to give way and then 'return to the charge', Bouquet laid down similar principles for the conduct of his own troops.

'Firstly, that the troops destined to engage Indians must be lightly clothed, armed and accoutred. Secondly, that having no resistance to encounter in the attack or defence they are not to be drawn up in close order, which would only expose them without necessity to a greater loss. And, lastly, that all their evolutions must be performed with great rapidity, and the men enabled by exercise to pursue the enemy closely, when put to flight, and not give them time to rally.'

ST. LUCIA

The value of light infantry is well illustrated by the action that took place at St. Lucia in the West Indies, in 1778, after the French intervention in the War of Independence. A few hours after the British had landed and seized the fortified naval base, and a peninsula known as Vigie Point in the northern part of the island, a strong French fleet arrived from Martinique. The French commander, Comte Jean Baptiste D'Estaing, then landed 12,000 men with the object of attacking the isthmus at Vigie Point and seizing the harbour. The British troops had to guard the island against attack from any direction so the force holding the isthmus itself consisted of only 1,300 under Colonel William Medows. Medows held back the bulk of his force in rear of the isthmus but sent five light companies to hold two wooded hills in advance of it. D'Estaing thought to brush aside these advance troops with an

French Colonial Infantry, 1772

attack by two battalions. To his utter astonishment, both battalions were badly mauled and thrown into confusion by the British light infantry who then successfully withdrew through a belt of brushwood before D'Estaing could cut them off. D'Estaing then launched his troops in heavy columns across the isthmus itself but his men were powerless against veterans trained in the American school, and they were twice beaten back. After three hours' fighting the British were down to their last cartridges and the order, 'cease fire' had been given. The British infantry had actually lowered their muskets when a gun captured from one of the French forts fired its last round straight into the French who were massing for attack. The French column wavered. An order rang out, and firing a last volley the British drove the French from the isthmus with the bayonet. The French infantry had had enough and ten days later D'Estaing withdrew his shattered forces back to Martinique. The British losses were 13 killed and 148 wounded, but the French casualties amounted to 400 killed and 1,200 wounded.

KING'S MOUNTAIN

The War of Independence brought into the ranks on both sides men who had learned from childhood to use a rifle and who had an instinctive understanding of the kind of tactics that had defeated Braddock's ill-fated regulars. Perhaps the finest example of American tactics occurred in 1780, when a mixed force of British regulars and provincial levies under Lord Charles Cornwallis was advancing in three columns into North Carolina. From the start of the operations, American irregular troops had harassed the columns, ambushing foraging parties, cutting the rearward supply routes and attacking detached posts. An advance detachment of 1,100 militia under Patrick Ferguson, who was one of the column commanders, had been drawn away some seventy

Backwoodsmen at King's Mountain

miles from the main force at Charlotte by news of one of these attacks. Suddenly Ferguson found himself confronted by a large force of several thousand settlers and was forced to withdraw. The backwoodsmen, realising Ferguson's dilemma, sent 1,500 hand-picked men to cut off his retreat and force him to give battle before reinforcements could arrive. Ferguson chose to make his stand on a hill known as King's Mountain. The hill itself was covered with trees, and the lower slopes were strewn with high boulders. On one side there was a precipice and the whole position appeared almost impregnable. The following afternoon about a thousand backwoodsmen arrived and having tied up their horses, started to move up the hill from three sides. Creeping up in complete silence, each man made his own way moving from boulder to boulder. When the central party reached the crest, Ferguson met them with a volley and a bayonet charge. The backwoodsmen fell back slowly, keeping up such an accurate fire from behind trees and boulders that the pursuit was held in check. Ferguson now found his men under a withering fire from a second party that was lying in wait on his right flank. Turning to face the new threat, Ferguson found that the third party of backwoodsmen, which had remained hidden on the opposite flank, was now firing into his rear. Thus entrapped, and with no room to manœuvre, the militiamen were up against overwhelming odds but they fought on until Ferguson himself was killed. Nearly 400 militia lay killed or wounded, and the remainder laid down their arms. The casualties amongst the backwoodsmen were eighty-eight. Sir John Fortescue, the historian of the British Army, comments on this exploit as being, 'as fine an example as can be found of the power of woodcraft, marksmanship and sportsmanship in war'.

THE BAKER RIFLE

It was not until the turn of the century that Colonel Coote Manningham was instructed by the Duke of York to form a corps of riflemen with an establishment of eight companies. A number of Hessian or Jaeger mercenaries had been used in the British Army in America and their short, thick-barrelled rifles and green uniforms were adopted for the new corps. Ezekiel Baker, the Whitechapel gunsmith, was given the contract (in 1800) for the rifles and produced a pattern to take the standard musket ball. This rifle, however, was very heavy and needed a wooden mallet to hammer down the ball; it proved very unpopular with the more experienced soldiers who had seen service in America. The standard pattern eventually adopted had a seven-grooved barrel with a bore of ·625 inch, similar to that of a carbine, and weighed about nine pounds. The barrel was two feet, six inches long and had a fore and back sight. The stock was well shaped at the 'wrist' and was fitted with a brass trigger guard which formed

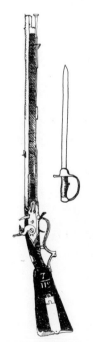

Baker rifle and sword bayonet

87

Rifleman of 60th Rifles with Baker rifle

a pistol grip. The left side of the butt was shaped to form a cheek rest and all these refinements were of course designed to assist the aim. Large butt boxes with brass covers held small tools (that screwed into the end of the ramrod) for extracting any balls that jammed and also for holding patches when these were used. The bayonet for the Baker rifle was twenty-three inches long with a flat, single-edged blade and a brass handle

88

with a knuckle bow which clipped on to a bar on the side of the barrel. The sword bayonet weighed two pounds and it completely upset the balance of the rifle when fired with the bayonet fixed. The adoption of the Baker rifle was a compromise as regards weight, range (300 yards) and accuracy, but the maximum rate of loading was one round per minute.

Corporal 42nd. Highlanders (the Black Watch)

Chapter Five

Nations in Arms

CONGREVE'S ROCKET

The principles of rocket propulsion were known long before the discovery of gunpowder. The earliest use of rockets in war is attributed to the Chinese who, by the thirteenth century, had developed a 'flying arrow', whose head consisted of a tube filled with an inflammable mixture. This idea of using a rocket to carry 'flying fire' into an enemy's encampment, or to harass his cavalry, appealed to the oriental mind, but in the Western world rockets were rarely made except to be used at a fireworks display to celebrate a coronation or a military victory. In India, in the 1780s, Hyder Ali and his son Tippoo Sahib, who led the Mahrattas against the British, both used rockets as a substitute for artillery. Tippoo indeed raised the number of the rocket-men in his army to no less than 5,000. The rockets themselves were made out of iron tubes about two feet long, and could weigh as much as twelve pounds. They were fitted to long bamboo poles, and were claimed to have a range of up to one and a half miles. The rockets were normally launched off an earth ramp, and to be effective, they had to be fired in salvos. As a result of these campaigns, the British Government decided to make large war rockets. Experiments were made at the Royal Laboratory at Woolwich by William

Congreve's rocket

Congreve, who later succeeded his father as Comptroller of the Laboratory. In 1805, Congreve produced the first efficient military rockets to be seen in Europe. The case was of sheet iron with a hollow spherical or cone-shaped head welded on to one end. The head could be filled with powder to act as a shell or left empty to be used as a shot. Several sizes were manufactured, the largest weighing twenty-four pounds. These large rockets could also be fitted with a special 'carcase' head, which was drilled with a number of vents and filled with a highly inflammable mixture containing saltpetre, sulphur resin and tallow. The bottom of the case, or tube, that held the propellant composition was closed by an iron disc which had five vents through which the gas escaped. After trials with a stabilising stick fixed to the side of the case, Congreve adapted the base-plate so that the stick would screw into a hole in its centre.

Congreve's rockets were first used for the naval bombardment of Boulogne in 1806 when eighteen ships fired some 200 small rockets into the port from a range of 2,400 yards and caused extensive damage mostly by fire. A similar, but considerably heavier, naval bombardment brought the surrender of Copenhagen the following year after the city had been virtually destroyed, again by fire. Used as a shell, Congreve's rocket had one great disadvantage. The fuse for the bursting charge was set in the base of the head, and

91

Rocket Troop in action

before the rocket could be used at short range, some, or even all, of the fuse compound had to be bored out with a tool inserted through the filling hole in the top of the spherical head—a lengthy and dangerous task. It may have been for this reason, and also because of their inherent inaccuracy, that Congreve's rockets were never popular with either the gunners or the infantry. Field carriages, portable frames, individual metal tubes fitted with flint-locks to fire the rocket, and even rocket guns to be fired from the shoulder, were all tried out. Many Continental armies imitated Congreve's rocket and from time to time they were used in minor wars. In 1844, William Hale perfected a rocket which was made to spin like a bullet, and consequently needed no stabilising stick. A hundred years later the rocket was re-discovered to become a major war weapon, taking many forms from the American anti-tank bazooka to the V1, the German flying bomb, while rocket ships capable of firing a thousand rockets in a single salvo prepared the way for amphibious landings in the Pacific and on the Normandy beaches.

Hale's Rocket

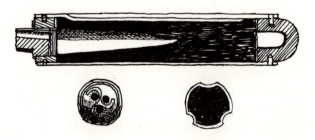

92

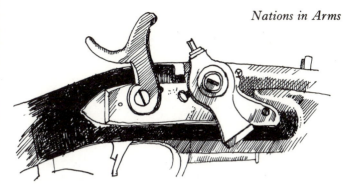

Forsyth's percussion lock

FORSYTH'S PERCUSSION LOCK

Many country parsons were dedicated sportsmen, but one who was also an amateur chemist and mechanic would be exceptional in any age. Such a man was Alexander Forsyth, a Scottish minister who evolved an entirely new method of igniting a powder charge. The great disadvantage of a flint-lock, especially to a sportsman, was the 'hang fire' time-lag between the flash in the pan and the explosion of the main charge in the barrel. Forsyth knew that fulminate of mercury exploded when it was struck by a hammer, and conceived a means of using this instantaneous action as a detonator in his sporting gun. By 1807, Forsyth had produced an entirely new kind of lock which could be fitted to any firearm. In the place of the priming pan there was a round plug screwed into the barrel along the top of which a channel led directly to the touch hole. A metal container or magazine shaped like a scent bottle fitted over the end of the plug. The lower part of the magazine held the fulminate powder, and the upper part was fitted with a plunger. When the magazine was swung upwards some of the detonating powder dropped into the cavity in the plug (there was enough powder for about twenty-five shots). The magazine was then turned back 180° to the firing position. When the hammer was released the blow was transmitted by the plunger which exploded the ful-

93

minate and the charge was fired instantly. Forsyth took his lock to London, and for a time worked in the Tower of London, supervising the manufacture of a lock suitable for military purposes. Later, he took out a patent and launched a private company for marketing his invention which was in some demand for sporting guns. Although Forsyth's lock was never adopted by the army, his invention led to a whole spate of experiments in the use of fulminates and the eventual discarding of the flint-lock.

In London and Paris, as well as in America, gunsmiths vied with each other to produce a 'primer' that would stand up to service conditions. Waterproof patches and tape strips (as for a toy pistol), pellets and tiny metal tubes filled with fulminate compositions were all tried out, and some were widely adopted. Of all the inventions the percussion cap was the most efficient. Projecting from the touch hole in the breech was a nipple. On this was placed a small copper cap containing fulminate. This priming system was simple, weather-proof and virtually fool-proof. The idea of neither the nipple nor the cap was new, but Joshua Shaw, an artist who left England for America where he succeeded in obtaining a patent for his copper cap, subsequently received $18,000 from the American Government as the inventor of the percussion cap. It was now only a short step before the invention of a cartridge which contained primer, powder and ball in one case, and the development of repeating and self-loading firearms.

CITIZEN ARMIES

Within ten years of the signing of the Treaty of Versailles, which brought independence to the American Colonies in 1783, Europe was plunged into war with Revolutionary France. The next two decades saw a transformation in warfare which was the direct result of the new concept of popular sovereignty. In America

Percussion Caps

the handwriting had been on the wall. The citizen army that had brought about the surrender of Lieutenant General John Burgoyne's redcoats at Saratoga had no counterpart in Europe, where war was the province of the hired professional. Philosophers, such as Jean-Jacques Rousseau, saw that in the defence of liberty and equality in a democratic state a citizen must be prepared to fight for his country. One French military writer, Comte Jacques de Guibert, whose *Essai de Tactique Générale* appeared in 1772, indeed forecast the use of a citizen army in a war of movement, with the troops living off the enemy's country. On 23rd August, 1793, the Revolutionary Government decreed a *levée en masse* under which all citizens could be conscripted into a national army. This single event heralded an age of unlimited war. In the nation's struggle for survival its whole resources of men and matériel had to be mobilised. In Napoleon, France now found a general to organise and lead the 'armed hordes' which for nearly a generation terrorised Europe.

NAPOLEON'S ARMY

Within a year of the decree of 1793 France had half a million men under arms and as further steps were taken to introduce national service the size of her armies grew. Under General Vaquette de Gribeauval, improved guns had already been introduced and the artillery made more mobile, but the other arms had to make do with old-fashioned weapons that could be

Soldier of French
Revolutionary
Army

mass-produced. There was no time to experiment. Nor was there time to train the raw levies in elaborate drills and manœuvres. Proud of their newly won independence, and spurred on by patriotic fervour, the citizen soldiers could be relied on to attack with enthusiasm, but only in their own way. Moving forward in a ragged order each man used what cover he could find. Then, regardless of losses, the assault was pressed home by fresh bodies of troops launched as close as possible to the enemy's line. For greater effect these attacks were made *en masse* by solid columns of men who rushed forward with astonishing speed. These tactics, mixing skirmishers and shock action troops, exemplified the spirit of Revolutionary France, combining the initiative of individuals with the emotional violence of the mob. With an almost inexhaustible supply of men thirsting to fight for their beliefs and for the cause of freedom, ideological warfare had returned to Europe.

The increased size of armies brought changes in organisation because a single commander could no longer control such numbers on the battlefield. The answer was found in the division, a self-contained force of some ten to twelve battalions of infantry, about six squadrons of cavalry and its own artillery, which was controlled by a single artillery commander, the battalion guns having been withdrawn. Divisions found their own outposts and marched and fought as a single formation, often being given an independent role such as finding an advance guard. The system had many advantages, as it allowed the army to advance on a number of parallel routes. This helped conceal the army commander's intentions and led to a strategy based on deception and surprise, as the divisions were so placed that they could either concentrate rapidly or threaten the flanks of the enemy. Freed from set procedures and orders of battle, the divisional commanders could use the three arms—cavalry, infantry and artillery—in the best combination according to the ground and situation of the moment. Much attention was given to cavalry reconnaissance and to the use of concentrated artillery fire to blast a hole in the enemy's line at the critical point of attack. Napoleon's genius, indeed, lay not in tactical innovations, or the use of new weapons, but in his flair for deceiving his enemy by the threat of flank attack so that his forces were divided. Then by a rapid concentration a crushing blow would be delivered on the weakened front.

CAVALRY

The Prussian and Austrian cavalry still held to the high standards of horsemanship and manœuvre set by Frederick the Great. Napoleon, who had been trained as an artillery officer, had a far less sophisticated view of cavalry training and tactics. The regiments were brigaded and formed into divisions and even corps. Weight of numbers and shock action replaced speed and manœuvre in attack and, always thirsting for

Austrian cuirassier

British dragoon in Wellington's Army

precise intelligence of his opponent's moves, Napoleon used the majority of his cavalry well forward in a broad arc reconnoitring and screening his own advance. The cuirassiers were usually kept in reserve to deliver a crushing blow at the climax of a battle. They wore steel helmets and both back-plates and breast-plates to protect them as much as possible from musket fire, as they were only trained to charge at the trot. They were mounted on huge horses and were armed with a long, straight sword, a carbine and a pair of pistols. The number of regiments of the Cavalry of the Line was greatly increased. These were dragoons who wore a green uniform with differently coloured facings for each regiment; their only armour was a brass helmet. They carried a sword, a cut-down musket thirty-seven inches long, a bayonet and pistols. Again, they were formed into divisions and employed in large numbers to provide a cavalry screen and carry out various protective duties such as holding the flanks. Under Napoleon they were increasingly used in battle as shock

French lancer in Napoleon's Army

troops in their true cavalry role, but in the fighting in the Peninsular War (1808–14) when the French were continually harassed by the Spanish guerrillas, dragoons were frequently used in a dismounted role and in the endless task of keeping the lines of communication open. It was the light cavalry, however, which was the most numerous and dashing part of the mounted arm. They were given the most exacting and arduous duties, particularly that of reconnaissance, and they invariably accompanied the infantry advance, flank and rear guards. Their whole training was directed towards rapid and aggressive manœuvres, so that in action they could harass and pin down the enemy by lightning attacks. In pursuit, their speed and dash often turned withdrawal into rout. 'These adventurous troopers,

99

the darlings of the ladies, wore the brightest and most extravagant uniform and were expected to maintain the highest standards of bravery and application on active service and the highest degree of swaggering bravado, boasting, swearing, gambling, and (less officially) duelling, on all other occasions.' The hussar regiments, who regarded themselves as the *élite* of the army, wore the most dazzling uniforms. They were often brigaded with the more numerous *chasseurs-à-cheval* and both were equipped alike, with sabre, carbine and pistols. To these were added several regiments of lancers, of which the most famous were the Polish and the Red Lancers, armed with the lance, sabre and a brace of pistols. A colourful addition to the Imperial Guard of picked troops that accompanied Napoleon wherever he went, and which constituted his ultimate reserve in battle, was a force of Mamelukes recruited after his conquest of Egypt. These retained their flowing robes and elaborate, oriental horse trappings and were armed with a scimitar and blunderbuss together with pistols and daggers.

INFANTRY

Napoleon expected his infantry to move quickly and whenever possible to live off the country. Tight uniforms were loosened, gaiters were shortened and the shako replaced the three-cornered hat. Coat facings were no longer ornaments, but made to button across to give a double protection over the chest. Tents were never issued, but each man carried a greatcoat and bivouacked in the open. The 1777-pattern musket was universally adopted. The bore was ·66 inch and with the bayonet it weighed eleven pounds, rather less than the Brown Bess which was five inches shorter, and of larger calibre. The French musket was useless over 250 yards and normally used at 100 yards or less. Each man carried fifty or sixty cartridges and three spare flints, which had to be changed after about a dozen shots. The musket barrels got so fouled up by the black powder that they had to be washed out every fifty rounds. The normal rate of fire was two rounds a minute.

Infantry divisions varied in strength but were organised into two or three brigades and each brigade had at least two regiments. Three or four battalions made up a regiment and within the battalion there was one grenadier and one light company and four fusilier companies. At full strength a company contained 140 officers and men. As the quality of the conscripts fell off, Napoleon came to rely more and more on *élite* troops. The grenadiers were formed into divisions and hand-picked men were enrolled into the Imperial Guard which in 1813 totalled 72,000 infantry, all experienced veterans or specially selected conscripts. No captain or subaltern of a line regiment was allowed a horse and the number of baggage animals was cut down to a tenth of those used in the Prussian Army. Marching behind their band the infantry pace was normally seventy-six steps, or 'paces', to the minute, but when called upon they were capable of amazing feats of endurance and speed. For instance, a division summoned from Vienna to join Napoleon at Austerlitz covered ninety miles in just over forty-eight hours. On the field of battle, the infantry moved at the quick step of 120 paces to the minute, or at the double. The training of Napoleon's infantry was based on three principles: mobility, skirmishing and the massed bayonet charge in column.

By comparison, the Prussian infantry were still trained in the rigid drill movements and, although one man in six was a light infantryman armed with a rifle, they were not at all good at skirmishing. It was only in open country, where their disciplined volley fire could be properly used, that they had any advantage. The French, on the other hand, continued to train the

Russian Infantryman: early nineteenth century

light company in each battalion as skirmishers, the men earning the title of *voltigeurs*, which means literally 'runners' because they were supposed to be able to keep up with trotting cavalry.

L'ORDRE MIXTE

A formation commonly adopted in Napoleon's army was *l'ordre mixte* which was a combination of line and column. As a regiment formed up to attack, the *voltigeur* companies from each battalion moved forward as skirmishers and the centre battalion took up its position in line ready for 'fire action'. On either flank the remaining two battalions were drawn up in column. The diagram shows the columns having a two-company frontage, so with eight companies drawn up in pairs the battalion column would have a front of fifty yards, and with the companies formed in three ranks, the column would be twelve ranks deep. The guns usually moved with the deployed battalion or sometimes on the flanks. Another favourite method of employing columns was for battalions to be formed in depth in two lines, but with sufficient space between the columns for the cavalry and guns to move freely to the front or flank. The advantages of column formation were that it facilitated this kind of mobility and was very flexible,

L'ordre mixte – Napoleon's attacking formation

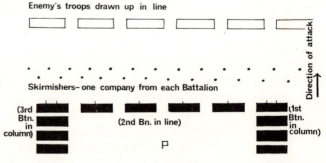

Enemy's troops drawn up in line

Skirmishers – one company from each Battalion

Direction of attack

(3rd Btn. in column)

(2nd Bn. in line)

(1st Btn. in column)

French Demi-Brigade of three Battalions

as the troops could change direction or form square to repel cavalry very quickly and without elaborate training.

LINE VERSUS COLUMN

For generations battles had been fought between armies formed in lines. Now, Napoleon's shock tactics with massed infantry had won him dramatic victories all over Europe. Not even the Prussian infantry could maintain their line against the bulldozer attacks of the French columns, with battalion after battalion thrown in at the same point regardless of losses. Would these tactics bring the subjugation of the whole of Europe? The Duke of Wellington certainly was unimpressed, but then he did not believe in Napoleon's maxim that victory went to the big battalions. In a small army like the British, the soldier was accustomed to facing long odds and almost overwhelming numbers. Discipline, training and morale were all important, but the ace card was the fire power of the British infantry. Against the French Wellington chose his ground with this in

British fusiliers formed in three ranks ready to repel cavalry
(only a small part of one side of the square is shown)

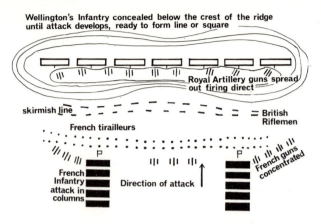

Line versus Column

mind so as to give his infantry every possible advantage in battle. The British line regiments fought in two ranks so that every man could use his musket to the greatest effect, but when a cavalry charge was expected the ranks were doubled or the order was given to form square. The drill to form line from square or vice versa was practised until the movements were absolutely automatic, as was the musketry drill itself. Ideally, Wellington placed his 'thin red line' just on the reverse side of a hill so that their ranks were protected from direct gun fire. If possible, the flanks were covered by natural obstacles, otherwise the cavalry were placed to protect the flanks. The guns were brought well forward, if necessary in front of the line, so as to fire on the enemy's lines of advance and break up any cavalry charge. If the enemy's cavalry were launched early in the action, the gunners would continue firing until the last moment and then run back into the infantry squares. The charge would be met by volley upon volley with the horsemen swirling round the squares and presenting an ideal situation for a counter-attack by the British squadrons. As soon as the danger had passed the line would re-form to meet the French infantry columns struggling up the rising ground with

104

quickening pace until the men began to run, shouting, '*Vive l'Empereur!*' and, '*En avant avec la baionnet!*' All this time the British line stood silent and motionless. Then, with the French less than 300 yards away came a single movement, a quarter turn, and the muskets were at the ready. Even now there was silence in the British ranks. Then their volley crashed out and

Private, Light
Company 3rd.
Foot Guards

the front ranks of the massed French columns would disintegrate as those behind reeled and staggered with the shock and crash of the discharge. Then, with three great cheers, the British would charge straight at their opponents who were already in disorder and unable to close their ranks. The charge was never pressed more than a few hundred yards before the British infantry calmly took up their original positions to await a further attack. This inevitably followed as soon as French reinforcements could be brought up and usually met with the same want of success and even heavier losses.

One of the secrets of Wellington's success was that in the opening stages of a battle he employed a powerful screen of light infantry to act as skirmishers, so that the French *tirailleurs* never got close enough to his main position to cause any serious damage. As soon as Wellington was given command of the British Army in Portugal he increased the number of companies of light infantry in each brigade for this very purpose, and soon afterwards, he created the celebrated Light Division. This became the protective screen for the whole army—a kind of strategic skirmishing line which kept off the French until the actual moment of battle,

Rifleman, Kings Royal Rifle Corps

and prevented them from discovering the dispositions of the main body of British. Employed as the advance or rear-guard for the army throughout the Peninsular War, the exploits of the Light Division became legendary, and Wellington's confidence in the riflemen of the celebrated battalions that formed the division was never betrayed.

THE COSSACKS

In the Russian Campaign of 1812, Napoleon suffered his first major setback. The long march to Moscow not only met with the most stubborn resistance but, in spite of elaborate preparations, the problems of supply became increasingly difficult. Supply convoys struggling over the atrocious mud roads were under constant attack, and often weeks and even months late, if indeed they ever arrived. Adopting a policy of 'scorched earth', the Russians destroyed houses, crops and cattle in the path of the French advance. Early in the campaign, Emperor Alexander I's army had been joined by over 30,000 Cossacks from the Ukraine and Caucasus, under their redoubtable leader Count Matvei Ivanovich Platoff. Born to the saddle, the Cossacks were the finest horsemen in Europe. Their mounts were small, well bred and capable of great endurance. Forced marches were made at a fast walk (of as much as five miles per hour) and at full stretch the horses could equal the swiftest chargers of any opponent. The Cossacks were armed with lance, sword and pistols stuck into a girdle or broad belt. They never used spurs, but had a short whip hanging from the wrist. Their confidence, both in their mounts and in their own skill as horsemen, and in the use of weapons, was such that before a charge each man would single out an opponent to engage in single combat.

It is often thought that the terrible winter conditions drove the French back from Moscow. Napoleon made

Cossack at the defence of Moscow, 1812

a fatal mistake when he decided to occupy what was
left of the city after three-quarters of it had been burnt
to the ground in the face of his troops. In this phase
of the campaign the Cossacks played a vital role.
Forming a cordon round the city, they occupied the
roads and attacked the supply columns. The French
cavalry, already seriously depleted, were forced to make

108

forays deeper and deeper into the countryside in search of fodder and were often cut off and captured. In a period of only three weeks over 4,000 French troops were lost in this manner, without a single battle being fought. To quote only one example of the difficulties that faced Napoleon at the start of the campaign: his cavalry had amounted to 80,000 horsemen, but when he abandoned Moscow there were only 15,000 cavalry horses left. Before the campaign was over, more than 200,000 trained horses (of the cavalry, artillery, and transport services) had been lost.

Day by day, as the French struggled back, the Cossacks harried the rear-guards, hunted down the stragglers, and made daring flank attacks, constantly forcing the weary French columns to turn and fight. One moment the Cossacks would appear as a black line on the horizon; then a sudden flank attack would come in with a cloud of horsemen pouring down on exhausted and starving men who turned to fight for their lives; the next moment there would be nothing to see but the birch trees and pines. But within the hour the manœuvre would be repeated; day by day the French ranks thinned and the stragglers never came in. Then the snow and intense frost came. But the Cossacks, seemingly immune to the terrible winter, still pressed their attacks, taking their daily toll of the remnants of the defeated French Army. In the six-month campaign which ended with the retreat from Moscow, the French lost half a million men.

Chapter Six

From Waterloo to the Crimea

After the defeat of Napoleon at Waterloo in 1815, there was a general revulsion against war and through the efforts of the great powers, acting in concert, peace was maintained for nearly forty years. With the exception of Prussia and Russia, who still maintained large forces, most states discarded conscription and slashed the size of their regular armies. For instance, the strength of the British Army in 1815 had been 685,000, but within six years it was down to 100,000 men, half of whom were virtually banished to the colonies. The lessons of the recent wars were forgotten; musketry practice was almost unknown, and all training was done on the parade ground. The ordinary private soldier, tied to the boring routine of life in barracks or serving long years in some remote corner of the Empire, was forgotten by the rest of the nation that was being swept forward by the Industrial Revolution towards a new era of trade and prosperity. Inventions, such as George Stephenson's locomotive, Robert Fulton's steamship and Samuel Morse's electric telegraph, that were to have such far-reaching effects on the economic and social life of the industrial nations, were later on to transform the whole pattern of Western warfare. British sea power was to become increasingly dominant, and by the middle of the nineteenth century, Continental powers were able to concentrate large armies through the use of elaborate railway systems. In the meantime, however, the great powers were engrossed in acquiring vast colonial territories and in expanding their trade, and were well content to allow their military forces to rub along as best they could. Nevertheless, this age of scientific discovery, which brought steam power to the factories and mills, and peaceful inventions, such as the sewing machine and electric bulb, equally brought discoveries of direct military application in the field of explosives, and in the design of guns and firearms. In the Prussian and French armies the process of modernisation was taken seriously as neither country was willing to display any military weakness. In Britain and the United States the case was very different. Although thousands of flint-locks were converted to percussion, little money was spent on developing new ideas which were often turned down out of hand, regardless of the results of tests. The superiority of the rifle over the smoothbore musket was indeed recognised, but in the British Army only the Rifle Brigade was equipped with rifled muskets. The re- mainder of the infantry up until late in 1854, well after the start of the Crimean War, were still armed with smoothbore percussion muskets, and in many cases, with the Brown Bess flint-lock musket, the manufacture of which had only ceased some ten years previously.

REVOLVERS

Flint-lock 'revolvers' with a cylinder loaded with from five to seven cartridges, using the same principle as Puckle's gun, had been in use for some time, but unless very carefully loaded and handled they were liable to premature explosion with disastrous results to the user. The first true revolver was made in 1818 by Elisha Collier, an American whose original patent was taken out in London. His first model used a priming magazine which filled each pan of the five-chambered cylinder as it

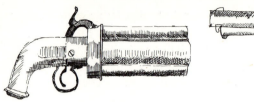 

Pepper-box pistol
Colt revolver

was rotated. When percussion caps were introduced, Collier fitted nipples to each chamber, and he also invented a mechanism which rotated the cylinder and locked it in position when the hammer was raised. At this same period there was a great vogue for 'pepper-box' pistols. These had a cluster of three or more barrels which rotated round a central spindle. In early versions, the barrels had to be rotated by hand and locked in place before firing; later the cocking of the hammer automatically turned and locked the barrels in position. Pepper-box pistols were muzzle-heavy, and so the barrels were made shorter and shorter which made them very inaccurate.

It was Samuel Colt, born in Hartford, Connecticut, in 1814, who produced the first really practical revolver. Although his first business venture to manufacture and market his firearms failed through lack of government support, in the end his revolvers were mass-produced in his own factory and sold all over the world. No single feature of Colt's system was entirely new but his revolver was a practical weapon of simple design and strongly constructed. He was granted patents, both in England and the United States, in the mid-1830s, when he was only about twenty-one. The principal feature of his design was an ingenious mechanism that rotated and re-locked the chambered breech in line with the barrel each time the hammer was cocked. Such a mechanism, where the hammer has to be pulled back manually before each shot, is known as 'single action'.

112

The first double-action revolver was produced by an Englishman, Robert Adams, a few years later. His revolver fired faster than the Colt because a single pull on the trigger both cocked the hammer and then released it. Single-action Colt revolvers were still being produced after the Second World War. This model was the Peacemaker or Frontier which was introduced in 1873, long after the death of Colt himself. When Samuel Colt built his armoury at Hartford in 1853, he set it up with 1,400 machine tools for the mass-production of small arms of all types. His example was soon followed in Britain, where a considerable quantity of the new machinery and technicians brought over from the United States were installed in 1855 at the Royal Small Arms Factory at Enfield.

THE BRUNSWICK RIFLE

The Brunswick rifle, originally developed in the 1830s by Captain Berners in Brunswick, was designed for quicker loading than the Baker rifle it replaced. The heavy barrel, which was thirty inches long, was drilled with two deep rifling grooves set opposite each other that made one complete turn in the length of the barrel. The rifle was originally designed to take a slightly oval-shaped ball, and it was thought that the smaller number

Brunswick rifle, showing notch in muzzle and belted ball

of grooves would reduce friction and speed up loading. The British version used a ball with a raised belt which fitted into the deep grooves. To help load the rifle at night, notches were cut into the muzzle to guide the ball which, complete with grease patch, was rammed down on the powder cartridge. The rifle was not only too heavy (weighing nine and a quarter pounds, plus two pounds when the sword bayonet was fixed) but the belt on the ball in fact increased the friction, and also led to excessive fouling. Worse still, it produced a wobbling flight of the projectile. The result was that the rifle was so inaccurate over about 400 yards and so difficult to load after a few shots had been fired, that it was reported as being 'the worst military rifle in Europe'.

THE MINIÉ BULLET

In France, a different technique was attracting much attention. A loose-fitting ball or bullet was dropped down the rifle barrel and then hammered against a narrow ledge or, alternatively, against a pillar in the breech chamber. This flattened out the base so it could grip the rifling. In both cases the bullet became distorted and there was excessive gas leakage and fouling. The real breakthrough in the design of rifle bullets came when Captain John Norton of the 34th Regiment of Foot started experimenting about 1820 with an expanding bullet. The idea was extremely simple. A pointed, cylindrical-shaped bullet, which aerodynamically was the ideal shape, small enough to slide down the barrel easily, had a hollow cavity in its base. The impact of the explosion forced the sides of the hollow base outwards to 'bite' into the rifling grooves. A similar model was produced by William Greener, a celebrated English gunsmith, who placed a small, wooden wedge in the hollow base of the bullet, and when the wedge was driven into

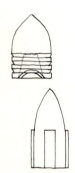

Rifle bullets, the Minié and (below) the Jacob 'shell'

the cavity by the firing of the charge, the same result was produced. In the late 1830s, the British Board of Ordnance tested both inventions and turned them both down! This simple idea is in fact in use in every rifled small-arm that has been manufactured in the last hundred years. It was left to Captain Claude Étienne Minié of the French Chasseurs to develop an almost identical idea, and to publish the result of his experiments in 1849. Taken up immediately by the French Govern-

114

ment, the Minié system was quickly adopted by the majority of the Western powers. The Minié bullet had three grooves filled with tallow and the cone-shaped cavity was plugged with a thin iron cup. The complete cartridge containing charge and bullet was designed to drop down the barrel easily. The rifling of the Minié rifle was shallow at the muzzle and progressively deeper towards the breech, an innovation which made the conversion of smoothbore muskets both cheap and safe.

BREECH LOADERS AND VON DREYSE'S NEEDLE GUN

The first breech loader to be issued in quantity was made by John H. Hall of Maine for the United States Army in 1819. In the Hall rifle the whole breech block and firing mechanism tipped up to load. In front of the trigger guard was the catch which held the block in the firing position. At about the same time a Swiss inventor, Samuel Pauly, was working on break-open breech, rather like the type used in the modern shot-gun. Pauly concentrated on preventing the escape of gases through the breech. He designed a new type of cartridge which had a tiny pan of fulminating powder in the centre of the 'head' of the cartridge, which is the end holding the charge. This part of the cartridge was made of soft metal and had a lip which fitted into the breech chamber. When the round was fired, the metal expanded tight against the walls of the chamber and stopped the gases blowing back. Pauly's gun had no hammer, and was fired by a firing pin. In a demonstration, Pauly fired twenty-two shots in two minutes, but his gun was considered too complicated for the raw French recruits to manage. Pauly's centre-fire metal cartridge case was never adopted in his lifetime, but all modern cartridges are made on the same principle and his invention made possible the development of automatic weapons in the second half of the nineteenth century.

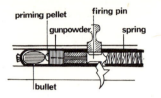

Dreyse's needle gun; diagram showing the path of the needle through the base of the cartridge

One of Pauly's assistants, Johann von Dreyse, who left Paris to return to his native Prussia, started a factory to make percussion caps. Von Dreyse developed a combustible cartridge with the percussion compound in the hollow base of the bullet. The firing pin was very long and thin so as to pass right through the charge and strike the primer—hence the name, 'needle gun'. In 1837, von Dreyse produced a new kind of breech which opened and closed like a bolt on a door. The Prussian army was re-equipped with Dreyse's bolt-action rifles in 1848. They were considered so superior to any other rifle in use that elaborate steps were taken to keep their construction a secret from other governments. The real value of von Dreyse's rifle was its ease of loading and its main disadvantage was that the needle broke after a few hundred rounds, through being subjected to intense heat and corrosion after each explosion.

THE JACOB RIFLE

The last rifled musket to be issued to the British Army was the 1853-patterned Enfield which, including the bayonet, weighed nine pounds, three ounces. The barrel had three grooves and was thirty-nine inches long, and the bore ·577 inch. At its trials this rifle proved accurate up to 800 yards. One of the most fascinating series of experiments going on at this time was being conducted, in what was literally an outpost of the Empire, by Major John Jacob who was commanding the Scinde Irregular Horse on the Indian frontier with Baluchistan. Entirely at his own expense, Major Jacob had several patterns of four-grooved rifles made in

Jacob's double-barrelled carbine

116

London and sent out in connection with his research. Jacob tried out various types of projectiles—a double-belted ball, a conical-shaped bullet with four studs to fit the rifling grooves and several kinds of explosive bullets. The rifle that he developed and unsuccessfully tried to get adopted for the army had an astonishing range and was sighted up to 2,000 yards. One of Jacob's more dramatic demonstrations with his rifle was to blow up a dummy ammunition cart over a mile away with his explosive 'shells'. After his rifle had been rejected by the army authorities (some say because it was considered too accurate by his superiors who only thought in terms of volley fire) he turned to perfecting a double-barrelled carbine with an extra-long bayonet, with which he equipped the two regiments of Jacob's Rifles that he himself had raised. John Jacob is remembered with great affection to this day in the district to which he brought peace, and which he administered so ably as political superintendent and commander of the frontier forces. After his death, the inhabitants of this remote frontier district insisted that their principal town, which Jacob himself had built, should bear his name—Jacobabad.

ARTILLERY

Within four years of Napoleon's defeat at Waterloo, the British artillery had been reduced to a quarter of its wartime strength, with skeleton batteries of only two guns each. By 1852, only two years before the outbreak of the Crimean War, the number of guns in the horse-artillery troops and field batteries had, however, been raised to six pieces in each case, but there were still only 120 guns in the whole of the field artillery. One significant difference, by comparison with the artillery that had fought at Waterloo, was an increase in calibre both of guns and howitzers. More howitzers were used in the field artillery and what were called position batteries had both 18-pounder guns and 32-pounder howitzers.

Lancaster rifled gun at the Siege of Sebastopol

These heavier pieces were less mobile than the field guns and were used in a more static role, and to strengthen defensive positions. The establishment of a field battery was four 9-pound guns and two 24-pound howitzers. All these were smoothbore pieces made of cast iron or bronze and, except for being of larger calibre, were virtually identical in design to the ordnance used in the Napoleonic Wars. In fact, muzzle loaders remained in use in the British service until 1866. In the Crimean War rifled guns were used for the first time. These were British Lancaster 68-pounders, with the bore drilled out into an oval shape which made one turn in 360 inches. They had a range of 2,600 yards and were considerably more accurate than any smoothbore of the same period. The Lancaster rifled guns and the heavy mortars which fired a 64-pound shell played a major part at the siege of Sebastopol, causing considerable damage to the fortifications and town itself.

PERCUSSION FUSES AND BOXER'S SHRAPNEL SHELL

The invention of fulminating powder led to the introduction of the percussion fuse for firing cannon. The fuse was ignited by a blow from a hammer which was fixed on the gun, the hammer being released by pulling a lanyard. Soon after this innovation, a friction tube was introduced. This was a very simple device. A small bar of roughened metal was set in the head of the tube which was packed with fulminating powder. A clean pull on the lanyard hooked to this bar set up the necessary friction to detonate the powder and fire the gun.

An improved type of shrapnel shell was invented in 1849 by Captain Edward Boxer of the British Royal Artillery who was made Superintendent of the Royal Laboratory at Woolwich. With the old pattern of shrapnel shell there had been many premature bursts, owing to friction between the powder bullets and the shell itself. Boxer's idea was to keep the bursting charge separate from the bullets by the use of what he called a diaphragm. He also invented a new kind of time fuse. This was made in the form of a wooden plug, with a centre channel filled with powder and a secondary channel which led down to the base of the fuse and thus direct to the charge. This secondary channel was filled with a fast-burning powder and into the side of the fuse a number of holes were drilled. These holes were filled with clay and covered with paper, which was marked with numbers representing fractions of time. To set the fuse one of these holes was drilled through so that the two channels were connected. The fuse was then placed in the shell which was now set to explode in the air after a certain length of time. When the shell was fired the powder in the centre channel started to burn and when the connecting hole was reached the flash passed down the secondary channel and detonated the bursting charge.

Friction tube

Boxer's time-fuse and diaphragm shrapnel

BAYONETS

The very long triangular-bladed socket bayonet continued in fashion so long as the Brown Bess was issued in the British Army. The obvious advantage of being able to fire with the bayonet fixed, however, was somewhat offset if the fore-sight was damaged by a tight-

119

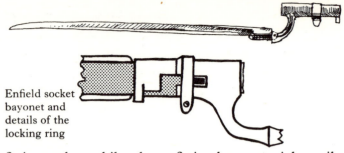

Enfield socket bayonet and details of the locking ring

fitting socket, while a loose-fitting bayonet might easily fall off. As late as 1843, during the Sind Campaign in India, the 22nd Regiment of Foot suffered the indignity of having their bayonets snatched off by the enemy and had to resort to tying them on. The problem was never satisfactorily solved until the Enfield rifle, with a bayonet socket which incorporated a special locking ring, was issued ten years later. Both the Baker and Brunswick rifles were introduced for the use of light infantry who, as skirmishers, would rarely need to fix bayonets, which in any case would hamper their movements in close country. The sword bayonet seemed to be the answer: a dual-purpose weapon for close-quarter fighting. The Brunswick sword bayonet had a cross hilt similar to that of the Baker and a 22-inch blade. It was fitted to the side of the barrel by means of a slot and locking ring in the hand grip, which fitted over a lug. By comparison with the socket bayonet of the same period, which weighed about thirteen ounces, the Brunswick sword bayonet was exceptionally heavy, weighing two pounds. An interesting dual-purpose weapon of this period is the socket bayonet with a *kukri* blade which was issued to the Gurkhas. Like the bayonets issued to the yeomanry regiments, which were more like swords, it was a poor substitute for the original weapon.

CAVALRY SWORDS

Kukri bayonet

In the British Army, the heavy cavalry continued to carry a straight sword with a 35-inch blade and a hatchet-shaped point which made it almost useless for

120

thrusting. Much more attention had been given to the design of a sword for light cavalry. At the turn of the century a new pattern with a curved blade, designed by Colonel John Gaspard Le Marchant, had been issued to all light-cavalry regiments. Le Marchant was a man of exceptional talents, a fine horseman and brilliant swordsman. He rose to command Wellington's heavy cavalry in the Peninsular War, where he was killed leading a decisive charge at the Battle of Salamanca in 1812. It is perhaps as the founder of the Royal Military College, which later moved to Sandhurst, that he is now remembered. Le Marchant's sword was really a sabre, but made as light as possible, and without the exaggerated curved blade of the scimitar-type swords found on the Continent. The blade measured thirty-two inches in a straight line with a curve of two inches from the line. The hilt had a simple knuckle guard and leather grip and the whole sword was well balanced and very light to handle. The last six inches of the blade served both as cutting edge and point, as the sword was as much for thrusting as delivering a cutting blow. After about 1830, the light-cavalry sword was fitted with a longer blade which only had a slight curve towards the point. In 1853, all cavalry regiments were equipped with the same type of sword. This had a straight blade, thirty-five inches long and one and three-quarter inches broad with a spear point and was officially described as 'essentially a thrusting weapon'.

Cavalry Swords (a) Light cavalry sword designed by Le Marchant (b) Pattern introduced in British Army in 1853

THE LANCE

There were no lancers in the British Army until after the end of the Napoleonic Wars. Early attempts to train men to use a 16-foot lance were soon abandoned, and a 9-foot staff of ash, impregnated with linseed oil and tar with a spear-shaped head, was adopted. Later, bamboo was used for the staff and the head was made with three sides like the bayonet of the same period.

121

A Zouave

THE YEARS BETWEEN 1815 AND 1854

Although there was no major war between 1815 and the outbreak of the Crimean War in 1854, there were numerous small wars and campaigns in widely separated parts of the world, and particularly in colonial territories. The French saw much fighting in Algeria, and the Russian Army was involved against both Turkey and Persia, as well as having to put down an insurrection in Poland, while the Americans, using a high proportion of volunteers to supplement their small regular army, defeated the Mexicans in the War of 1846–48 which brought California and Texas into the Union. The British Army faced increasing responsibilities in many parts of the Empire and the list of minor wars and campaigns in which its scattered units took part is almost endless—in Nepal, Ceylon, Burma, Afghanistan, China, South Africa, New Zealand and many parts of India. Four out of five line regiments were serving overseas and some regiments remained abroad for as long as twenty-five years without returning to England. By comparison, the French Army was far less extended.

The *chasseurs-à-pied* saw a good deal of service in Algeria and were converted to light infantry, being armed with rifles and sword bayonets. Regiments of Zouaves were also raised for service in Algeria. It was originally intended that they should contain a majority of Africans, but later each battalion had only one native company. The Zouaves wore a distinctive uniform, similar to their native dress, and were issued with rifles. They were constantly in the field and under their hand-picked officers soon gained a great reputation for efficiency and dash. The remainder of the French infantry were not issued with rifles until after the Crimean War and as regards tactical formations continued to use both column and line. The Prussian Army reverted to close-order drill in three ranks as the best means of training their short-service soldiers. Unlike the British, who were spread in penny packets all over the world, the Prussian Army was able to hold manœuvres and try out new tactical formations. Infantry regiments now deployed in company columns with the flank companies providing skirmishers. This gave the company commanders much more independence of action. The Prussian cavalry was increased but in other European armies the number of cavalry regiments was reduced for reasons of economy. Both in Russia and Austria cuirassiers were abolished and the proportion of light cavalry increased.

THE CRIMEA

While Britain and France were steadily developing their colonial territories in Africa and Asia, Czar Nicholas I of Russia picked a quarrel with the Sultan of Turkey over who should administer certain holy places in Palestine, then part of the Ottoman Empire. What the Czar really wanted was an outlet through the Bosporus into the Mediterranean so that he could threaten the Balkan countries and dominate the British route to India. Fear of Russia's obvious intention brought both Britain

123

and France to Turkey's aid, and both countries sent troops to Bulgaria to guard against a Russian advance on Constantinople. Although this danger was averted through the efforts of Turkey alone, Britain and France decided to mount a joint expedition against the Russian naval base and fortress of Sebastopol on the Crimean peninsula, a totally unnecessary operation for which neither army was really equipped or prepared. Nothing was known of the Russian defences and the troops were to be landed over an open beach, without land transport or any regular supply system or proper medical arrangements, to lay siege to a fortress of unknown strength, while their rear was exposed to attack from the mainland. Furthermore, during the months of waiting over 10,000 men had already died of cholera and many more were seriously weakened by the disease. However, the Russians were caught by surprise and the landing was unopposed. Marching down the coast towards Sebastopol, the two armies soon came to the River Alma, where 33,000 Russian infantry with 120 guns and 3,400 cavalry under the command of Prince Alexandr Sergeevich Menshikov waited on the far bank. The combined forces of the Allies, which included a Turkish contingent, were a good deal stronger in infantry than the Russians, and the field artillery amounted to 136 guns, but the only cavalry contingent was 600 British light cavalry. The Russians occupied a strong position and were so confident that they could hold the river line for several weeks that they had invited a number of ladies to view the fighting and had not bothered to entrench themselves on the rising ground behind the river.

The British Commander, Lord Raglan, and the French Commander in Chief, Marshal Saint-Arnaud, came to an agreement that the two armies should attack side by side. They had, however, no adequate maps, no knowledge of the Russian strength or where the river crossings could be made, and no concerted plan; neither issued any orders once the attack was started.

Allied Infantry in the Crimea

The brunt of the fighting fell on the four British divisions, each of about 5,000 men, that attacked straight across the river in two lines. The French who were attacking on their right nearer to the coastline waited for their guns and took little part in the battle until towards the end. The Russian artillery failed to stop the British battalions who advanced under fire for over a mile through vineyards and a burning village to reach the river bank. Still maintaining some semblance of line, more by instinct than through the efforts of the sergeant majors, the men struggled across intent only on closing with the enemy. The Grenadier Guards had marched shoulder to shoulder down the banks and into the river still in step and after they had crossed, some swimming and some wading, the right-hand man of each company (known as the company right marker) was called forward and the battalion was dressed again in two rigid ranks before the advance was again sounded. All the time grape-shot and cannonballs cut into the ranks. Part of the Light Division reached the main Russian battery

125

British Grenadier and Russian Infantryman (in winter uniform)

position in a shallow redoubt but was thrown back by
sheer weight of numbers. The battle between the ragged
British line and the heavy Russian columns went on for
three hours. The fighting was confused and bitter with
no quarter given. The Russians had expected to clear
the field with the bayonet; they were met by disciplined
musketry fire from men trained to fire and re-load as
they advanced. Now the British gunfire began to bite
into the Russian reserves moving forward, and with the
appearance of the French, who had scaled the cliffs near
the mouth of the river, the Russians abandoned their
remaining positions and retreated on Sebastopol. The
Russians lost 5,700 men, including five generals and
nearly 200 officers. Allied losses amounted to 2,300,
which included 1,400 British wounded who were
evacuated by sea to a hospital in Scutari at the head of the
Bosporus. Of these, more than half were to die, not of
their wounds, but of diseases actually contracted in
hospital. Seventy-five per cent of the total British
casualties in the entire war can in fact be attributed to

126

this single cause, and but for the devoted work of Florence Nightingale and her gallant band of nurses, this figure would have been even higher. In the bitter winter months that followed, the British suffered the most terrible privations from the lack of such obvious equipment and stores as tents and fuel and even greatcoats, as well as forage for horses. All this was reported by William Russell of *The Times*, who became the first proper war correspondent. By the end of the war the supply and medical services had some semblance of proper organisation, but Britain's neglect of her army through forty years of relative peace had taken a terrible toll in suffering and men's lives. It was a year before the fortress of Sebastopol was captured. One Russian attempt to break the siege led to the Battle of Balaclava, a battle remembered not only for the episode of the 93rd High-

Heavy mortar bombarding Sebastopol

landers and the 'thin red line', but also for the equally heroic action in which the light-cavalry brigade was sacrificed in a futile charge against Russian batteries 2,000 yards away. Later that same day, 3,000 Russian cavalry were driven from the field by the heavy-cavalry brigade who were outnumbered four to one. The Russian squadrons were formed in a solid mass and made the fatal mistake of remaining halted to accept the charge of the British dragoons who crashed into their close-packed ranks from three sides.

Trooper, 11th Hussars
in the Crimea

Chapter Seven

The First Modern Wars

The Crimean War, fought with the tactics and many of the weapons of an almost forgotten generation, marked the end of an era and a turning point in the history of warfare. Three wars in Europe, and a Civil War in America, followed in quick succession during the next seventeen years, and during this time far-reaching changes in weapons and tactics took place. Many influences were at work, and many inventions were to play their part: gun cotton, dynamite and smokeless powder for gun and rifle ammunition; a process for converting iron to steel; and the introduction of 'iron clad' warships. Submarine cables bridged the oceans, and the electric telegraph followed the vast network of railways that not only linked industrial centres, but became the means of moving and concentrating armies at a speed never before possible. Towards the end of the century Gottlieb Daimler's petrol engine and Rudolf Diesel's internal combustion engine, together with the invention of wireless telegraphy by Guglielmo Marconi and the first flight of an airship constructed by Count Graf Ferdinand von Zeppelin, demonstrated the coming of a new scientific and technical age. In this industrial age, there was a massive rise in population throughout Europe, and increased nationalism. Military thought was greatly influenced by the writings of the Prussian

General Karl von Clausewitz, who had died in 1830, but whose book *On War* is studied to this day. His philosophy was one of total war and the total involvement of the nation. In the last resort, he felt, military strength must be based on economic strength, and warfare itself would tend to become increasingly violent. Instead of the elaborate manœuvring and avoidance of pitched battles of an earlier age, generalship had to aim at the destruction of the opposing armed forces and this implied direct attack by large, concentrated armies. These theories were soon to be put into practice by Prussia, but in the meantime, the development of new weapons and manufacturing processes had resulted in an arms race between the major powers.

CARTRIDGES

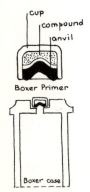

Boxer primer
and cartridge case

The paper-wrapped cartridge continued in general use until about 1865, by which time, largely as the result of the Civil War in America, many different patterns of breech-loading rifles were in production. To achieve an effective gas check in the breech, brass or copper cartridge cases of various design were being used and Colonel Edward Boxer, working at Woolwich Arsenal, had already designed a centre-fire brass-cased cartridge for the British Snider rifle, using a Minié-type bullet. This cartridge had a new kind of primer which incorporated what was called an 'anvil' in the base. This allowed the case to be easily re-loaded and used over and over again. This invention was quickly adopted in America and the Boxer primer is now the only kind manufactured for conventional small-arms ammunition in the States.

SMOKELESS POWDER

The invention of two new explosives, nitroglycerine and nitrocellulose, commonly called gun cotton, led to the

130

development of a smokeless and far more powerful type of gunpowder. The result was that bullets became smaller and more streamlined, to take advantage of high muzzle velocities, and the cartridges became long and slim. There was no longer a cloud of black smoke to obscure the firer's aim and give away his position. A more rapid rate of fire became possible, and the art of concealment part of a soldier's training. Just as the development of metal cartridges is linked with the adoption of breech-loading rifles, so the invention of smokeless powder speeded up the development of magazine and repeating rifles.

BREECH-LOADING RIFLES

Over a period of some twenty years, during the 1850s and 60s, dozens of breech-loading systems were invented. One of these was invented by Jacob Snider, who won a competition in 1864 for the cheapest and best way of converting muzzle loaders, and whose model became the first breech loader on general issue to the British Army. The breech block was simply a trap door, hinged on the right-hand side, which allowed the cartridge to be loaded when it was 'flipped' open. The original hammer of the percussion lock was retained and the blow was transmitted by a striker in the breech block which detonated the centre-fire cartridge. Another type

Breech of Snider Rifle

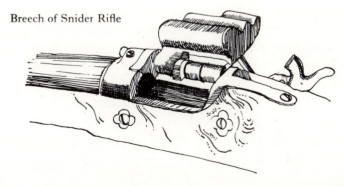

of breech block was hinged at the back and worked by a lever, usually the trigger guard, so that the cartridge could be loaded down the curved slope of the breech cover straight into the chamber. A variation was the Remington rolling block which opened upwards by a flick of the thumb when the hammer was cocked. Meanwhile, bolt-action rifles were being perfected. In one type, the straight backward and forward action of the bolt allowed the cartridge to be loaded, and the head of the bolt to be turned so as to lock in position ready for firing. This idea was used in the Ross rifle, later adopted by the Canadian Army, and also used by the famous Royal Canadian Mounted Police. The second, and more usual type of bolt action, was similar to that already used on the needle gun, in which the head of the bolt was locked against the chamber by the bolt itself being turned down. The best example is in the German Mauser. The bolt is in one piece with front-locking lugs and an extra lug at the back for safety. The single-shot Mauser replaced the needle gun in the Prussian Army in the 1870s. The bore was ·433 inch with four flat rifling grooves and the rifle with bayonet fixed weighed 11·6 pounds. The Mauser was sighted up to 1,750 yards which was about 550 yards more than most rifles in use at that time. It now needed only a short step forward to invent a repeating rifle that fired a number of rounds before it had to be re-loaded.

REPEATING RIFLES

In 1848, before centre- or rim-fire cartridges were introduced, Walter Hunt, an American whose many

Winchester repeating-rifle mechanism

Mannlicher's box-type magazine and clip

inventions included a fountain pen and a new sewing machine, produced a special bullet and a magazine rifle to fire it. The bullet had a hollow base to hold the charge, and a number of these fitted into a tube underneath the barrel of the rifle. The bullets were pushed down by a coiled spring and loaded into the breech, one by one, each time the lever action was operated. This basic idea was developed into the famous Winchester repeater which took fifteen rim-fire cartridges, loaded through the side of the frame. A simple down-and-back movement of the trigger guard loaded the cartridges in turn and cocked the hammer ready to fire. In a later model the lever action was replaced by a wooden hand grip which could be 'pumped' backwards and forwards to do the same job. The tube magazine was quickly taken up by other countries but a revolutionary type of magazine was soon to take its place. This was simply a metal box with an internal spring in its base which held the cartridges exactly in position ready to be loaded, one by one, each time the bolt was pushed forward. The normal backward-and-forward motion of the bolt at the same time ejected the empty cartridge case and cocked the action ready for the next round to be fired. It remained only for the Austrian inventor Ferdinand Mannlicher, in 1885, to introduce a special clip which held the correct number of cartridges ready to re-load the magazine in one simple, rapid movement. This simple device has been used by all magazine repeating rifles ever since.

Mitrailleuse

MACHINE GUNS

From about 1850 onwards, a number of inventors,
particularly in America, became fascinated by the
possibility of speeding up the process of loading and
firing by mechanical means. In the days of the muzzle
loader, battles had been won by infantry who could
load and fire more quickly than their opponents. Breech
loading and metal cartridges again placed the emphasis
on quicker loading and inventors began to dream of
machines that would produce the fire power of a whole
platoon, or even company, of men. A 25-barrel volley
gun produced by Dr Joseph Requa, an American,
looked rather like a fourteenth-century 'organ' gun.
Steel cartridges, with a hole in the base, were spaced out
in a clip ready for loading. The sliding breech was
closed by a lever and a trail of powder was run into a
channel behind it. When the powder was set off by a
percussion cap all the barrels fired simultaneously. A
team of three men could fire seven volleys a minute, but
the Requa gun was a clumsy substitute for aimed fire
by riflemen, and its principal use was for guarding
bridges where the enemy might be expected to bunch
together. A rather similar idea had been developed by
the Belgian firm of Montigny in the 1850s. Napoleon III
believed he had found a 'secret weapon' to use against

the Prussians, and an improved pattern was manufactured in great secrecy and issued to the French Army
in 1869, the year before the Franco–Prussian War broke
out. This *cannon-à-balles* or *mitrailleuse* had twenty-five
barrels set up in an iron tube. The cartridges were
carried in boxes of twenty-five and were loaded into the
breech by means of a steel plate, bored with holes, that
corresponded to the five rows of five barrels. A lever
closed the breech and the turn of a handle operated a
series of firing pins to produce slow or rapid fire. With
experienced loaders this gun fired up to 300 rounds a
minute. The *mitrailleuse* was mounted on a carriage
and looked like a field gun. The French made a grave
mistake, as we shall see later, by treating it as a piece of
artillery, instead of a heavy and rather clumsy multi-
barrelled rifle.

THE GATLING AND GARDNER GUNS

When the Civil War in America broke out, Richard
Gatling, who came from North Carolina, was a successful
manufacturer of agricultural implements, but he was
soon to become famous all over the world as the inventor
of the first proper machine gun. Instead of using clips
or plates to hold the cartridges, Gatling used a hopper,
or trough, fitted immediately above the breech mechanism, an idea already tried out on the single-barrelled
Agar gun, nicknamed the 'coffee mill' from the shape of
the hopper sticking up above the barrel. The prototype
Gatling gun was patented in 1862. It had six barrels set
in a frame which was rotated round a central spindle by
turning a crank handle. Each barrel had its own bolt
and firing mechanism operated by a cam, and the
cartridges dropped, one by one, into the open breech
as it passed below the hopper. In each complete revolution of the six barrels, each barrel was loaded and fired,
and the empty metal cartridge case was ejected. So the
faster the crank handle was turned the faster the gun

135

Gatling gun on field mounting

fired. Steel chambers, fitted with percussion caps, were used in this original model to hold paper cartridges, and these were fed into the hopper by hand. The Union General Benjamin Franklin Butler used twelve of these guns at the siege of Petersburg, Virginia, and after the end of the war a much-improved model, using copper rim-fire cartridges, was officially adopted for the American Army. For many years Gatling continued to work on improving his gun, and by the 1880s a 10-barrelled version, fitted with special circular feed cases, was firing 1,200 rounds a minute. Ten years later, an electrically operated model achieved a nominal rate of 3,000 rounds per minute, compared with the 350 rounds per minute of the original model.

Like the *mitrailleuse*, the Gatling was mounted on a wheeled carriage, and the tendency was for batteries to be formed under the command of the artillery. As the gun was liable to jam it was never popular with the British Army. Several Gatlings, however, were used in the Zulu War of 1879, doing considerable execution

136

against the massed attacks of those formidable, but poorly armed, warriors. The first really portable machine gun was invented by an American Army officer, Captain William Gardner. The original Gardner gun had several fixed barrels fed from a vertical box, but, after a number of trials, Gardner produced a single-barrelled version which used a clip to hold the cartridges. The rate of fire was either single shot or 120 rounds per minute. A feature of the Gardner gun was the alternative tripod mounting which enabled it to be used on a parapet, and also for the gun and tripod (which together weighed less than 220 pounds) to be carried on a horse. The Western powers were slow to see the true potential of machine guns, but the Gatling was sold to a number of Middle Eastern countries, as well as to China and Japan. The Russians manufactured their own copy of the Gatling, and used this in the war of 1877–78 against the Turks, particularly in two siege operations. Although heavily outnumbered, the Turkish infantrymen, with their superior breech-loading rifles, put up a very stubborn defence, and the Russians used their Gatling guns to cover their costly mass frontal attacks. Curiously enough it was the Royal Naval Brigades—fighting on land at the Battle of Alexandria in 1882, and later on in the Sudan, and on the Upper Nile—that proved that their Gatling and Gardner guns were best employed as

Gardner gun on tripod mounting

infantry weapons, and not as field guns. Within a few years the first real automatic machine gun was in service, and this remarkable invention, the Maxim, will be described in the next chapter.

BREECH-LOADING GUNS

One of the greatest steps forward in the development of artillery equipment occurred immediately after the end of the Crimean War. A Scottish civil engineer, who was later knighted to become Sir William Armstrong, invented an entirely new type of rifled gun. It was built up of several layers of wrought iron 'shrunk' onto an inner tube. This made the barrel immensely strong. The unique feature of the Armstrong gun, however, was a simple and virtually foolproof loading system using a falling vent-piece (or breech block) held in place by a breech screw which itself was bored out so that the shell and charge could be loaded directly into the chamber. In 1859, the Royal Artillery adopted the Armstrong 12-pounder field gun and a 9-pounder for the Royal Horse Artillery. Within a few years 40- and 64-pounder guns with side-opening breech blocks were also in production. The Armstrong shell was lead-coated so that the whole of the shell became a driving belt. The Armstrong 12-pounder was of 3-inch calibre, weighed 912 pounds, and had a range of 2,100 yards. Sir Joseph Whitworth, whose steel works and arms factory were in Manchester, also produced a new type of 12-pounder gun. This had a

Whitworth breech-loading mechanism

different type of breech which had to be completely unscrewed before the shell, which was specially shaped to fit the hexagonal rifling, could be loaded. The Whitworth 12-pounder had a maximum range of 3,000 yards and saw service in the American Civil War, where it was also used as a muzzle loader. The Whitworth gun, however, was not considered so reliable as the Armstrong and was never adopted for the Royal Artillery. Rifled artillery pieces now were generally accepted. In Britain, however, there were many advocates of the smooth bore who even argued that rifled guns were too accurate! The real changeover to breech loaders came in the 1880s as the result of several factors. The use of slower-burning powder and copper driving bands, which eliminated studs on the shell case, increased the muzzle velocity and led to longer gun barrels. This made muzzle loading very difficult and by comparison breech mechanisms had greatly improved. The Armstrong breech-loading mechanism had led the way and many countries were now in the race to convert the whole of their artillery to breech loading.

This spate of inventions, combined with new techniques for mass production, brought an arms race between the leading military powers, but the full potential of such weapons as the machine gun and breech-loading artillery was not immediately appreciated, and changes in tactics were even slower to follow. In the Italian War of 1859, Napoleon III came forward as the champion of 'Italy for the Italians' in alliance with the Sardinians against Austria. Rifled field guns were first used by the French in this war. Also, several French corps were moved forward by railway, but unfortunately no one bothered to see that sufficient supplies were also moved up. In the end the veteran French infantry, long experienced in Algeria, proved too much for the Austrians, but the tactics used on both sides were of a by-gone age. Attacks were made in column covered by skirmishers, and as far as the French were concerned, were largely led by the *corps élite*, such as the Imperial Guard and the *chasseurs-à-pied*. After the war, Napoleon III issued a directive that in defence, 'useless fire of skirmishers will be avoided; and while the deployed battalions engage in file-firing, the other battalions will beat the charge and attack the enemy with the bayonet'. But the Prussian Army, whom the French now began to look down on as 'little better than a militia', learned other lessons from this war.

THE AMERICAN CIVIL WAR

The war which broke out in America in 1861, between the Union forces of the Federal Government in the North and the Confederate forces of the Southern States, has been called the 'first conflict of the techno-logical age'. When the Union invaded the South they were faced with fighting over the territories of the fourteen seceding states, an area of 800,000 square miles or half the size of India, and well over 2,000 separate engagements and skirmishes took place. At one time there were one and a half million men serving in the opposing armies, and in a single month's fighting in Virginia in 1864 the Union lost 70,000 men.

The small regular army remained loyal to the Federal Government, except for 286 officers, out of about 1,000 West Pointers, who resigned to join the Confederates. Both sides, initially, had to depend on volunteers, although a form of conscription to meet the 'quotas' was later introduced—'a reversion to the democratic principle of the nation in arms'. The militia were almost com-pletely untrained—the average annual training often consisted of a one-day muster parade—and other regiments had to be raised from scratch. The supply of weapons and equipment of all kinds was totally inade-quate. Some Springfield rifled muskets using Minié bullets were in Federal stores, but the Southern States only had an assortment of Jaeger rifles and ancient flint-locks, stored since the Mexican War, or even the frontier days. Quantities of firearms were purchased abroad, particularly by the South, but many of these were of more or less obsolete patterns, and it was a long time before they could be replaced from factories that had to be built before production could be begun. The supply of ammunition for all the different calibres and types became a problem that was never really solved. For instance, two years after the war had started, the Union Army had over 100 different types of rifles, carbines and muskets in service use. Basically, the infantry of both sides were armed with muzzle-loading muskets or rifles and bayonets, although the latter were sometimes thrown away as useless impediments. The Union cavalry started the war with the Sharps single-shot breech-loading carbine, but later on were equipped with the Spencer 7-shot repeater. Southern cavalry had to make do with sporting rifles and shot-guns until carbines could be bought. Compared with a rifle, the cavalry carbine was outdistanced by several hundred yards. Officers carried revolvers and many troopers followed suit. In theory, the cavalry of both sides were armed with sabres, but in the South some regiments went short because there weren't enough to go round.

The Union field artillery was equipped with the bronze 12-pounder smoothbore Napoleon and the 10-pounder rifled Parrott gun, both of which were muzzle loaders. The Parrott gun was a cast-iron piece, reinforced with an extra band of wrought iron sweated on round the chamber and many different sizes were manufactured up to 10-inch fortress guns. Large mortars were also used, and one known as the 'Dictator', which took part

Spencer carbine breech mechanism

141

Heavy mortar on railway mounting

in the Siege of Petersburg, was carried on a railway truck and threw a shell weighing 220 pounds over two and a half miles. The Confederate field guns were mostly muzzle-loading smoothbore 6-pounders and 12-pounder howitzers, many of which had been captured early on in the war. A few heavier guns, British Whitworth and Armstrong rifled breech loaders, were purchased from abroad.

A feature of the war was the almost reckless manner in which field guns were pushed forward, even amongst the skirmishers, to assist the attacks. Little shrapnel was used, and the guns were often fought at 'canister range'. In the great areas of heavily wooded country, guns were at a disadvantage and used in small numbers, but in more open country it was found that massed guns could achieve dramatic results. At the Battle of Malvern Hill, the Federal Army fought a rear-guard action to cover their retreat from in front of Richmond, the Southern capital. Nearly 300 guns covered the gentle slopes leading up to the entrenchments near the crest of the hill. The Confederate attack was launched somewhat prematurely, before all their own guns were in position and the reserves assembled, and their infantry were beaten back with heavy loss. On the third day of the Battle of Gettysburg, 159 Confederate guns were massed against the centre of the Union position occupying Cemetery Hill. In preparation for an infantry attack, Confederate batteries pounded away as fast as the guns could be loaded, seeking out the infantry positions on the ridge. Slowly, some ninety Federal guns took up the challenge in an unequal duel. After about an hour the Federal gun fire died down. In the belief that the opposing batteries had been silenced, and realising they had little ammunition left to support the actual attack, the Confederates launched ten brigades of infantry on a front of a mile. But the Federal guns had ceased fire solely to await such an attack, and soon great gaps were being blown in the advancing lines. The American military historians, Colonels Ernest and Trevor Dupuy, describe the scene:

'As the Confederates came on, apparently oblivious of the carnage strewed behind them, more and more Federal artillery pieces joined the fight, until more than two hundred were pouring destruction across the narrow stretch of open farm land. Now the Southerners were within musket range, the Union infantrymen, who had been watching this scene with dreadful admiration, lost themselves in the familiar routine of battle. The leading Confederate line stopped, fired a volley, then rushed on towards the crest and the smoke-covered Union entrenchments.'

The flanks of the attack now came under a withering fire, and although the attack went through on the centre to gun positions on the crest of Cemetery Hill, there were too few survivors to beat off the counter-attack. 'Back down the slope of Cemetery Ridge came the survivors, the long, orderly formations broken into confused clumps of men. Some were running, but most were walking, sullenly, defiantly.' At the Battle of Gettysburg, over 180,000 men were involved, and the fighting lasted three days before the Confederates withdrew, having lost a third of their force. The cost to the Federal Army,

Skirmish line and deployment of infantry in attack

however, had been nearly as great, one man in four having been killed or wounded.

As the war dragged on, fire power was seen to dominate the battlefield, and the range and effectiveness of the rifle and the field gun dictated tactics, both in attack and defence. In defence infantry were entrenched or protected by breastworks. Reserves were held back under cover where they would be relatively immune from shell fire. The spade and the axe became more important than the sword or the bayonet. Infantry attacked in a succession of skirmishing lines, with the men spaced out to avoid the long-range rifle and gun fire. As the range closed some would give covering fire, while others rushed forward in a series of leap-frog rushes. But the defence still retained the advantage and as far as the infantry was concerned there was little tactical manœuvring, many battles becoming a slogging match between defenders in entrenched positions and a series of attacking waves, fed by reserves, attempting to force the issue at close quarters.

Cavalry tactics were mainly dictated by the nature of the terrain which was largely wooded. Although the cavalry of both sides charged with the utmost determination whenever there was the opportunity, such occasions were rare, and generally speaking they fought as mounted infantry and often on foot. The war, however, proved without any doubt the value of independent cavalry, organised in large formations such as the division, which proved invaluable for outpost duty, for scouting, and for reconnoitring and gaining intelligence of the enemy's movements. In particular, there were

Entrenchments and wire entanglements in American Civil War

many instances of cavalry raiding deep into enemy territory as well as operating against the lines of communication with considerable success.

Of the many outstanding cavalry commanders in this war probably the most remarkable was the Confederate Major General Nathan Bedford Forrest, a former slave trader who had started out in the war as a private soldier. It was typical of this tall, energetic and quite fearless man that in his very first action in command of a volunteer regiment he succeeded in ambushing and putting to ignominious flight an armour-plated gunboat carrying nine heavy guns that had been sent to destroy a stores depot on the Cumberland River. Early

Cavalry trooper –
American Civil War

on in the war, while raiding in Tennessee, he came on a stores depot guarded by Federal infantry. His own force, which included some light artillery, totalled 275 men. The Federal troops were driven from their positions in a spirited cavalry charge and retreated into a small fort, which they had strengthened with a breastwork of cotton bales and hogsheads of tobacco. Forrest withdrew his men to cover and ordered dismounted action with the guns in support. Faced with a hail of well-directed small-arms and artillery fire, the garrison of 400 surrendered. The spoils of war amounted to 1,000 horses and mules, 20 wagons, and hundreds of thousands of rounds of gun and small-arms ammunition, as well as quantities of equipment and stores. In the Battle of Tishomingo Creek, Mississippi, in the summer of 1864, two strong lines of Federal infantry charged three of Forrest's regiments who were dismounted and holding a defensive position. In spite of well-directed carbine fire the attack was pressed home, but at thirty paces the Confederate cavalry drew their revolvers and repulsed the assault with heavy loss. The horses were led forward and the Federal withdrawal soon became a full retreat. Harassing action by the cavalry continued for two full days, by which time the Federal troops had been driven back fifty-eight miles. In this action Forrest's force of 3,200 men was outnumbered three to one, and the Federal losses were 1,900 dead and over 2,000 prisoners, plus 19 guns, over 200 wagons and large quantities of supplies. The Southerners originated the employment of cavalry as mounted riflemen and were very successful until the Federals had learned their system and in time, with their superior resources and overpowering numbers, beat the Confederates at their own tactics.

In what other ways was the American Civil War different than any that had preceded it? Firstly in the involvement of the ordinary man and woman through the raising of large volunteer armies, which in turn made increasing and urgent demands on the industrial and

Hand grenade
(detonated by
percussion caps)

146

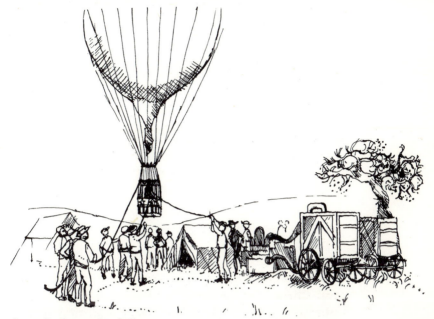

An early observation balloon

economic capacity of the nation as a whole. Then there was the successful use of railways to move and supply troops over great distances, and the organisation of railhead depots and a forward supply system. Above all there was the extraordinary inventiveness displayed throughout the four years of struggle. Magazine rifles and the Gatling gun have already been mentioned. Armoured trains and observation balloons were used; mines and booby traps, grenades and rockets of ingenious design were tried out, as well as the use of wire entanglements. Finally, through the introduction of the field telegraph and Morse signalling by lamp and flag, commanders were able to control larger forces in the field than ever before.

Laying a field telegraph cable; American Civil War

Chapter Eight

A Time for Change

THE FRANCO-PRUSSIAN WAR

It was now the turn of two great European powers to experience modern warfare. Otto von Bismarck, 'the Iron Chancellor', Prime Minister of Prussia under Wilhelm I, had for years been using war, first against Denmark and then against Austria, as a means of unifying the German peoples under Prussian leadership. Now Bismarck was to take on France. Helmuth von Moltke, the Prussian Chief of the General Staff, a brilliant and dedicated officer, had for years been preparing plans for the mobilisation and deployment of the army. Von Moltke saw that railways would play a vital role in any future war. Strategic railways were constructed and a new Department of the General Staff was formed to take complete charge of the lines of communication. All that was needed to launch a fully trained and equipped army, backed by a most thoroughly organized system of supply, was the issue of a single code word and the setting of a date. Within eighteen days of the outbreak of the Franco–Prussian War in 1870, Prussia had mobilised 1,183,000 trained men (including the *Landwehr* or reserve army which consisted entirely of ex-regulars) and had assembled three armies totalling 462,000 men on the French frontier. By comparison, French preparations had come too late. Two years previously the legislature had reluctantly

Krupp's heavy gun in action; Franco–Prussian War

agreed to introduce a system of partial conscription to increase the size of the French Army. Those who escaped the call-up were to do two weeks' annual training over a five-year period in the Garde Mobile. These measures were half-hearted and completely unrealistic. For instance the Garde Mobile only trained for a day at a time and when war came, had little equipment and less organisation. Shutting their eyes to the reality of Prussian preparations for war, the French legislature kept cutting back military expenditure, and six months before the outbreak of war, were even proposing to reduce the next call-up by 10,000 men.

Prussia's easy victory over Austria in 1866 had been largely due to the superiority of its breech-loading needle guns over the muzzle loaders of its opponents. The French hurriedly introduced the Chassepot, a single-shot bolt-action rifle which had a long firing pin. The sabre bayonet issued with the Chassepot had a 22-inch blade. The latest type of muzzle-loading rifles also were converted by cutting out the breech and fitting a hinged breech block which swung open to load and extract. This was called a *tabatière*, in other words, a snuff box. The Chassepot, with a range of 1,200 yards,

149

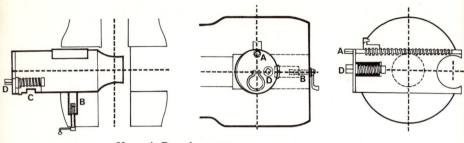

Krupp's Breech system
Left: Horizontal section (Wedge Open)   Centre: Side view
Right: Vertical section (Wedge Closed)
A. Screw for moving wedge in and out
B. Catch pin to hold wedge when closed
C. Nut or recess for catch pin
D. Screw for tightening wedge

gave the French infantry a decided advantage over the Prussians, but unfortunately war broke out before some units could be properly trained in its use. The Prussians on the other hand had a large number of breech-loading rifled artillery pieces, which were much superior to the French muzzle-loading bronze cannon. The Prussian artillery, in fact, was thoroughly up to date, and a steady flow of new breech-loading steel guns had been coming from the Krupp factory, near Essen, to re-equip the Prussian Army and also to be sold to Russia. Two years before the Franco–Prussian War broke out, a British officer had reported that the Krupp factory already covered 450 acres, and employed 8,000 men, with many more working at the nearby coal mines and blast furnaces. By this date the factory's output had already exceeded 3,500 guns with a further 2,200 on order for immediate delivery. The breech-loading system was based on a semi-cylindrical wedge which was stronger and easier to operate than other contemporary systems.

In the Franco–Prussian War many of the lessons of the Civil War—which, surprisingly, von Moltke dismissed as no more than 'two armed mobs chasing each other around the country, from which nothing could be learned'—went unheeded. The French realised the effectiveness of the breech-loading rifle and relied on breaking up the Prussian attacks before delivering a counter-stroke. Their opponents, however, who had an identical doctrine of counter-attack, still launched their infantry attacks in columns, and only later began to use skirmishing formation. King Wilhelm had in fact refused to alter the drill manual, issued nearly twenty-five years previously, and clung to manœuvres in battalion column, 'as a necessary corrective to the tendency to loose order'.

In a battle fought just west of the fortress of Metz two significant actions took place. The French, with four corps under Marshal Achille Bazaine (112,800 men and 520 guns), occupied good defensive positions on a ridge stretching from the village of St. Privat to a spur which overlooked a deep, wooded ravine and the village of Gravelotte. The German attack was made by two armies—the First Army under General Karl Friedrich von Steinmetz, an elderly but distinguished officer, and the Second Army commanded by Prince Friedrich Karl; the whole force totalled 188,332 men and 732 guns. Von Moltke, as the King's Chief of Staff and sole advisor,

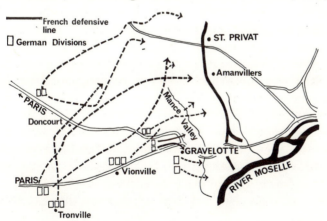

Battle of Gravelotte and Saint Privat

ordered von Steinmetz to attack through Gravelotte, while Prince Friedrich Karl marched on Amanvillers, which was thought to be the right of the French position.

The approach from Gravelotte rose steeply up through the wooded ravine towards the French entrenchments and gun emplacements along the crest and was also commanded by several walled farms, which had been loopholed and turned into strong points. One of these, the St. Hubert farm, directly looked down on the narrow road, which climbed up through deep cuttings. The German attack towards Amonvillers was repulsed; one of their officers later wrote, 'The grating noise of the mitrailleuse was heard over the tumult drowning the whole road of battle.' Meanwhile, Steinmetz's troops had come into action. From above Gravelotte, 150 guns began to pound the French entrenchments and a battery of *mitrailleuses*, which was too far forward in an exposed position. When the German infantry debouched from the ravine they presented easy targets as, still bunched together, they struggled up the steep slopes. Supports and then reserves were thrown in, but, after several hours of fighting, the only German success was the capture of the advanced post of St. Hubert. Here a concerted rush by no less than fourteen companies had finally broken into the farm. Convinced he was only opposed by rear-guards, Steinmetz threw in the infantry of his second corps, all his reserve artillery and a cavalry division. With the main French positions still intact, the result was disastrous. The infantry advancing from the ravine were within 800 yards of the French entrenchments and the attack was met by the fire of 200 guns and *mitrailleuses*, while the whole crest blazed with the deadly fire of the Chassepot rifles. A few German guns reached St. Hubert only to be knocked out one by one. The remaining batteries ordered forward never struggled clear of the village which was being steadily shelled by the French.

In the ravine, the cavalry became enmeshed in the struggling mass of infantry. A single regiment managed to break through up the slope but was met with a hail of bullets and thrown back with terrible loss. Only two hours had elapsed since the fall of St. Hubert, and the scene in the ravine and the village of Gravelotte was one of utter confusion and chaos. The infantry of yet another corps were thrown in on the orders of the King himself. Again the attack was repelled and panic began to spread. In the growing darkness a large group of German infantry crouching amongst the ruins of St. Hubert were fired on by fresh troops attacking from the rear. Some units were pressing forward, while the remnants of others were streaming back. Groups of infantry and cavalry, gun teams and riderless horses, and a stream of wounded filled the constricted space. Ahead, a wall of smoke rose from 144 French guns now in action. Above, a column of dust darkened the sun and still the shells crashed down, the bursts echoing through the trees. And now the Germans were streaming back along the congested road, followed by the whistle and swish of the bullets that seemed to come from either side. Now was the moment for a French counter-attack, but Bazaine could only think of holding on to his defensive position and was too far back to control the battle.

Meanwhile, further north the German advance had been checked opposite the village of St. Privat, which, it was now realised, was the key position on the right flank of the French Army. The village was solidly built with a number of walls and hedges on its outskirts which

Prussian infantryman

gave good cover for a succession of firing lines. Beyond it the ground fell gradually away for a considerable distance over fields which gave practically no cover. Prince Friedrich Karl ordered the Saxon Corps to march round and take the village from the flank, while the Guards Corps waited for this attack to start before launching their own direct assault. Meanwhile, no less than 180 guns were assembled and opened fire. Within an hour the French artillery had been overwhelmed and could do nothing to stop the shelling of St. Privat, where some nine French battalions waited amongst the crumbling walls and burning buildings. When the French gunfire died down, Prince Friedrich Karl allowed the Guards Corps to send forward three brigades to take the village, without waiting for the Saxons, or even arranging covering fire. First a line of companies, with skirmishers pushed ahead, stepped out into the open and then came into sight the thick infantry columns, each of half a battalion, marching steadily across the bare fields towards their objective a mile away. The French skirmishers had lay hidden all day, 600 yards in advance of the village, and now opened a steady and deadly fire. As the range closed, the main body of defenders, formed on the outskirts of the village, sent a hail of bullets into the close-packed German ranks. Practically every mounted officer was shot down. 'The men on foot struggled forward against the Chassepot fire as if into a hail storm, shoulders hunched, heads bowed, directed only by the shouts of their leaders and the discordant noise of their regimental bugles and drums.' By the time the attack had reached the French skirmish line, all semblance of order had been lost, and the ragged line of survivors was driven to ground by the murderous fire from the village. Every movement brought a rain of bullets. No advance was possible against such accurate and devastating fire. Over 8,000 officers and men had been lost in not much more than twenty minutes.

The village fell later that evening to a combined assault by both the Saxon and Guards Corps; some fifteen battalions and a further fourteen batteries of artillery were used for the assault. While the gallant French commander, Marshal François Canrobert, succeeded in extracting much of his force, the Germans were too disorganised to follow up the retreat. Some idea of the storm of fire to which they had been subjected may be judged from the fact that Canrobert's infantry had, in two days' fighting, fired two million cartridges, as many as the Prussians had expended in the whole of the war of 1866 against Austria. Overnight the French Army withdrew towards the fortress of Metz. Their losses were around 12,300, but the Germans had suffered heavily. Over 20,160 officers and men was the cost of their massed attacks, which only on the extreme right had eventually penetrated the French defences. Only the Germans' superiority in artillery and Bezaine's failure to counter-attack at Gravelotte had given them their costly victory.

CAVALRY

The employment of cavalry in this war is of special interest. Both sides retained heavy cavalry for shock action. Cuirassiers, armed with sabre and pistol, represented one-fifth of the French cavalry force, but the Germans increased this proportion of heavy cavalry to two-fifths by adding a large number of Uhlan regiments. The French lancers who were armed in a similar manner with lance, sabre and pistol were used as light cavalry. Otherwise the light cavalry on both sides, whether dragoons, hussars or the French *chasseurs*, were armed with a carbine and sabre. The French Chassepot carbine with a range of 800 yards was a much better weapon than the German needle carbine. While both sides kept back a reserve of cavalry for shock action, the French still thought in general terms of sweeping charges of an

Prussian Uhlan

155

earlier age, while the Germans had taken great pains in training their cavalry for reconnaissance and outpost duties in co-operation with the infantry divisions. Consequently, a cavalry division was allocated to each French *corps d'armée*, while the Germans put a regiment to work directly with each infantry division. From the very outset, the German cavalry demonstrated their superiority, being handled with great boldness. A party of Uhlans slipped across the frontier within days of the declaration of war to blow up a railway viaduct at Saargemünd, and a young staff officer, Count Zeppelin, who later invented the Graf Zeppelin airship, with a small patrol spent thirty-six hours many miles behind the French lines reconnoitring routes for the invasion of Alsace-Lorraine. During the advance from the frontier the German cavalry formed a protective screen twenty to thirty miles ahead of the marching columns. Unlike the French, whose cavalry were particularly inept at reconnaissance and outpost duty, the Germans were thus able to anticipate almost every move of their opponents and concentrate their army in secrecy behind an impenetrable cloud of mounted men. Such tactics enabled the Germans to close in on the French flank and rear immediately before the Battle of Sedan. Moving up through wooded country, which the French had not bothered to reconnoitre, the Germans surprised a complete French corps, encamped and cooking their meal.

French chasseur

The German shells falling amongst them was the first warning of the impending assault, which drove the French across the Meuse with the loss of most of their guns and all their baggage and stores.

During the war the cavalry of both sides attempted on several occasions to charge the opposing infantry. Towards the close of the Battle of Sedan the whole of the French reserve cavalry, amounting to nearly three divisions, was thrown in against the extreme flanks of a German attack in a last desperate attempt to save the day. The charge broke through the skirmish line, but the deployed battalions in the rear stood firm. No attempt was made to form square, but little knots of infantry opened fire at about 100 yards' range and simply mowed down the horsemen. Shortly after the battle, an officer wrote, 'The question of cavalry charging infantry with breech loaders, is, I think, settled conclusively by this campaign,' and his opinion of the charge at Sedan was, 'They were shot down before they could get within fifty yards—it was a useless purposeless slaughter . . . it had, practically, no result whatever.' After the French defeat at Sedan, the German cavalry were kept occupied guarding communications during the great sieges of Paris and Metz. This was the period when the French partisan bands, or *Francs-tireurs*, did their utmost to harass the invader, fighting with great bravery. It is an interesting comment on the employment of the Uhlans against these guerrillas, that German infantry battalions had to march alongside the cavalry to clear villages and close country, as without carbines Uhlans were virtually immobilised by the *Francs-tireurs*.

In military terms the lessons of the Franco–Prussian War were that the field gun had now begun to challenge the domination of the rifle, and the rifle had ended the long reign of the cavalry charge. Above all, future wars would be between 'nations in arms'. With the increased size of armies the Continental powers now turned to conscription, and the development of rapid-fire pre-

157

cision weapons. With these trends came the need for a large and efficient general staff, as a superior commander in the field could no longer lead in person, but must command through a staff large enough to handle all the complex details of modern war between large armies.

MAGAZINE RIFLES

The first magazine rifle adopted by the British Army was the Lee–Metford, first issued in 1889 and named after the two inventors responsible for its design. It weighed nine pounds, eight ounces, and with the sword bayonet fixed, was just over five feet long. The calibre was ·303 inch. Two sets of sights were fitted. The somewhat cumbersome backsight had graduations up to 1,900 yards and an 'extreme range sight' was fitted on the left side of the rifle, marked for ranges up to 3,500 yards. The magazine held eight cartridges and the rifle was fitted with a 'cut off'. This allowed single rounds to be loaded by hand. The rifle had been designed for use with the new smokeless cartridges, but it was found that they caused excessive wear and corrosion to the Metford barrel, which had seven shallow grooves. A new barrel with five deep grooves was designed at the Enfield factory and the rifle became the Lee–Enfield. Within ten years a lighter version with a shorter barrel was introduced and issued to both cavalry and infantry regiments. This Short-Magazine Lee–Enfield with only minor modifications remained in use through both world wars. The SMLE rifle (without bayonet) was only just over forty-four inches long, and weighed a pound and a quarter less than the original Lee–Enfield. The magazine took two clips of five cartridges and the particularly smooth bolt action enabled a high rate of fire to be maintained. The SMLE was introduced into the British service shortly after the Boer War and great care was taken over the sighting. A simplified, but more efficient leaf backsight, which also incorporated a wind

Lee-Metford rifle

158

Early Maxim
machine gun

gauge, was graduated from 200 to 2,000 yards, and could
be set for any intermediate fifty yards, and adjusted to
give two inches of elevation per hundred yards. By
comparison, the German 7·92-mm. Mauser which was
used throughout the Great War, was nearly fifty-three
inches long, and weighed nine pounds, twelve ounces.
The Mauser was an accurate rifle, but the magazine only
held five rounds, and the bolt action was very awkward
for rapid loading and firing. The first French rifle to use
smokeless cartridges was the Lebel, which weighed nine
and a quarter pounds. It had a tube magazine below the
barrel which held eight cartridges, but later (in 1907)
the Mauser-type magazine was adopted to take a clip
of three cartridges. It was only in 1916 that the magazine
was enlarged to take five cartridges. The *épée* bayonet
had a straight, quadrangular blade, twenty inches
long.

THE MAXIM MACHINE GUN

Hiram Maxim, an American of Huguenot descent, was
a man of outstanding inventive genius. From the age of
fourteen he had worked at many trades, accumulating
experience of both mechanical and electrical engineering.
By the age of forty he was earning the then very large

salary of $5,000 a year as an established expert in gas and electric lighting. The first electric lights used in New York City, in fact, had been manufactured by his company. Travelling on business to Paris and Vienna, he found that many of his business contacts were much more interested in ideas for developing rapid-fire weapons than in his own electrical inventions. On reaching London he set up a workshop in Hatton Garden to work on an idea that had come to him many years before. The terrible kick of an old Springfield rifle had made him wonder how this energy could be put to some useful purpose, instead of just bruising the firer's shoulder. After experimenting with a sprung-butt plate that re-loaded and cocked a Winchester rifle each time it was fired, he quickly evolved what was to become the first fully automatic machine gun. The very first model that Maxim constructed was so perfect that the design of his machine gun remained virtually unchanged throughout its long life of over seventy years. Maxim's gun fired at the rate of 600 rounds per minute and caused an absolute sensation. A demonstration was arranged for the Prince of Wales, later King Edward VII, and for the Duke of Cambridge. The little workshop in Hatton Garden became the meeting place for a whole stream of senior officers and officials from the War Office, and the firm of Vickers was commissioned to take over the production of what became known as the Vickers machine gun. But Britain was not the only country to realise the tremendous potential of Maxim's invention, and in 1888, the year that the gun was introduced into the British Army, the Kaiser saw the Maxim demonstrated at the Spandau arsenal in Germany, and gave orders that it should be adopted also for the German Army.

Charles ffoulkes, formerly Master of the Tower Armouries, describes the principles of the Maxim, which in one form or another, has been copied by every army in the world.

'The breech mechanism is operated by hand to insert the first cartridge into the barrel, the trigger is then pulled to fire the cartridge, causing the barrel to recoil. During the recoil, the breech is opened, the empty shell extracted, the firing pin cocked, and a cartridge brought into position and pushed into the barrel. The force of the recoil stores up energy in a spiral spring which returns the barrel to the firing position, inserts the cartridge, and closes the breech. The gun is automatically fired as long as the trigger is pulled. The cartridges (250) are fitted to a webbing belt moving from right to left. The barrel is cooled by a water jacket.'

The original calibre of the Maxim was ·75 inch, but the version used by the British fired the standard ·303-inch cartridge. A number of heavy-calibre (37-mm.) Maxims, firing a one-pound explosive shell and known as 'pom-poms', were used by the Boers as mobile artillery in the South African War. The Vickers Medium Machine Gun which proved itself in both world wars needed at least three men to bring it into action. The folding tripod mount weighed fifty-two pounds, and was a particularly difficult load. The gun itself weighed thirty-three pounds, but was ten pounds heavier with the water jacket filled. A single belt of ammunition weighed about fifteen pounds.

THE HOTCHKISS MACHINE GUN

Meanwhile, several American firms were already in the world market for automatic weapons. One such company

Hotchkiss
machine gun

161

started by Benjamin Hotchkiss had, at the time of his death in Paris in 1885, factories in Austria, England, France, Germany and Russia. A design for a gas-operated machine gun invented by an Austrian officer, Baron Adolf Odkolek von Augezd, and developed by the Hotchkiss company was adopted by the French Army in 1897. Large quantities of an improved version were sold to the Japanese. The principle on which the Hotchkiss machine gun worked was extremely simple. Gases escaping through a 'port' in the underside of the barrel drove a piston back with a hammer-like blow that operated the breech and firing mechanism. The heavy barrel was air-cooled and had thick radiating surfaces in the form of rings near the breech. A metal clip holding thirty cartridges was fed in from the left-hand side. The gun itself weighed fifty-four pounds, and the tripod about the same.

ARTILLERY

Breech loading and fixed ammunition, with the charge contained in a brass case just like a rifle cartridge instead of silk cloth bags for field guns, had speeded up loading, but the rate of fire was still about six rounds per minute. The problem was how to control the recoil. Fortress or

French 75mm
field gun

162

Erhardt field gun

naval guns had heavy stable mountings, but field guns jumped back and had to be re-laid after every round. The French were the first to use a hydraulic buffer to absorb the recoil and re-equipped their army with the famous 75-mm. field gun in 1896–97. Their secret was closely kept for a number of years, but the British were fortunate enough to discover a German engineer in Dusseldorf, a certain Herr Erhardt, who had invented a recoil system similar to that of the French 75. Without the German government realising what was going on, a number of Erhardt 15-pounder, quick-firing guns were manufactured and shipped over to England in plain packing crates, marked 'Machinery and Explosives', and issued to the regiments stationed at Aldershot. The gun itself rested on a cradle which was fitted to the carriage. When the gun fired it slid back along the cradle and the shock was taken up by a hydraulic buffer before the gun was returned by 'recuperator' springs. The carriage itself remained perfectly steady, and a coin placed on one of the wheels would not shake off when the gun fired. The sights and elevating gear were fitted to the non-recoiling portion so the gun-layers could follow the target continuously and the whole team keep close to the gun, instead of having to stand back every time it fired. Not only did the Erhardt model produce more rapid and accurate fire, but the gun team could now be protected by an armoured shield. Within months of being issued with Erhardt's guns the average battery

163

had learned to maintain fire at twelve rounds a minute and for a 'burst' twenty-eight rounds a minute, compared with the previous maximum rate of fourteen rounds a minute. The development of other types of artillery had lagged behind. Field howitzers were temporarily out of fashion, and the use of heavy guns, except as siege weapons, was unknown. In the South African War of 1899–1902, however, the British learned many lessons at the hands of the Boers. As far as artillery was concerned they were forced to adopt a completely new doctrine for the use of field guns and to re-equip the whole of their artillery as soon as the war was over.

THE BOER WAR

The British aspirations to extend Imperial rule throughout Africa had for years been resisted by the Boers, the Afrikaans-speaking descendants of the early Dutch settlers. Open war broke out in 1899, and lasted for two and a half years. The early Boer successes came as a complete shock to the British public. The problems of dealing with large-scale guerrilla operations were quite unexpected, and the army seemed powerless to conduct mobile operations against an elusive and cunning enemy,

Mounted Boer

British Colonial
mounted
infantryman

whose mobility, initiative and unorthodox tactics came
as a revelation to the more organised and disciplined
regular troops. The Boers, tough, hardy and independent, could call on every single able-bodied man to
join in the defence of his land and beliefs. Almost to a
man they were mounted on well-trained, wiry ponies
and carried Mauser rifles. In all, 90,000 men enrolled
but probably not more than half were in the field at any
one time. The Boers were natural marksmen with the
rifle, and had an instinctive sense of minor tactics. In
particular, they were complete experts in the art of
concealment, using every boulder or hummock or patch
of tall grass both in defence and attack. Where cover was
sparse their deep, narrow trenches, carefully camouflaged with vegetation, were so skilfully sited and
camouflaged that they were almost impossible to spot
even through field glasses. The British were faced with
subjugating territories which were as large as France
and Germany together. Their own bases at Capetown
and Durban were over 1,000 miles apart and the
country between mostly consisted of wide plains broken
by *kopjes*, which were small, round, peaked hills that

dominated the surrounding rock-strewn veldt. The few railway lines provided the only means of communication and the railway bridges the only means of crossing the broad rivers, except at fords or 'drifts' which invariably had steep and difficult approaches. The dispatch of an army corps brought the strength of the British regular troops in South Africa up to 70,000 men, the largest force ever to be sent overseas. Before the war was ended 450,000 British and Colonial troops and auxiliaries had been committed. The British infantry found themselves no match for the Boers at skirmishing and in set-piece attacks suffered very heavy casualties from the concealed marksmen, whose smokeless cartridges never gave their position away. When the field artillery tried to come into action in the open, as they had been taught, to engage the enemy batteries before supporting the infantry attack, the regular gunners suffered the humiliation of being shelled by dispersed and concealed guns and pom-poms which were almost impossible to spot, and which, because their positions were constantly being moved, were very difficult to knock out. The Boers used their limited number of modern heavy guns, mostly imported from Germany, with great skill and cunning

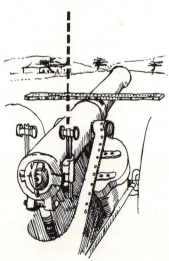

A 'Gunner's arc'
for indirect
artillery fire

and at ranges of up to 10,000 yards. Although few casualties resulted, marching columns were often forced to deploy prematurely and British guns were made to open fire at an unseen enemy at extreme range. There was now a call for more field howitzers and a larger issue of shrapnel and the field artillery were forced to improvise means of indirect fire. First, an improvised wooden scale, called a Gunner's arc, was fastened to the barrel. Later, a German-designed 'lining sight', looking rather like a sundial with a sighting arm, was used. Both enabled a target to be engaged from behind cover. The gun was laid by sighting onto a nearby fixed object while an observer, on higher ground, and in signal communication with the gun team, gave corrections to the line of fire by ordering for instance, 'right three degrees'. This simple instrument for measuring angles was the fore-runner of the dial sight used in the Great War. There was also an immediate call for accurate range-finding instruments, and for signallers who only the year before had been struck off the battery establishment. As field telephones were in their infancy and 'still under consideration' by the War Office, much use was made of amateur signallers with a knowledge of semaphore.

The Boers at the outbreak of hostilities had taken the offensive in Natal and within two months had succeeded in driving the British back into Ladysmith and also laying siege to Mafeking and Kimberley. Some 10,000 British troops were locked up in Ladysmith for ten months before the near-starving garrison was relieved, at the fourth attempt, by General Redvers Henry Buller, whose relief force by then amounted to 35,000 men. The Boers in the whole of Natal mustered no more than 27,000 men. The Boer Commander, Louis Botha, who was covering the siege operations, gave an earlier relief force a sharp lesson at the Battle of Colenso. The British troops had been hurried into the attack with insufficient reconnaissance and their guns, deployed within range of the Boer outposts, came under heavy rifle fire. The Boers

167

had little difficulty in beating off the attack with heavy
casualties and captured ten out of the twelve guns. The
next attempt to relieve Ladysmith also failed. The battle
took its name from Spion Kop, a boulder-strewn
saucer-topped peak which seemed to dominate the Boer
positions. The mountainside could be seen to be steep,
and in places, precipitous, but no one stopped to think
why the Boers had not attempted to mount their guns
on such a commanding position. The summit was taken
with the bayonet in a night attack with the loss of only
three men wounded, but the next day over two British
battalions found themselves pinned down in an area of a
few hundred square yards. Unable to dig in owing to the
stony ground, the troops were subjected all day to a
withering rifle fire, often at almost point-blank range, and
were continuously shelled by pom-poms and heavy guns.
The dispatch of more and more reinforcements merely
increased the number of British casualties on the
summit, where more than 4,000 men were now pinned
down. Unknown to the British, the Boers had already
drawn back, realising they could inflict greater losses by

A Heliograph
and a signalling
lamp in South
Africa

shell fire and sniping than in any attempt at hand-to-hand fighting. Communications on the British side had completely broken down. Messages from the only heliograph still working had taken up to four hours to be relayed from distant peaks, and no attempt had been made to lay a field telegraph line to the battalions on the summit. When darkness fell, only one signalling lamp could be found, and the oil gave out in less than three hours. The only man who had climbed Spion Kop to find out the true situation had been young Winston Churchill, who was with the force as a war correspondent. By the time he had gone back a second time with a message that the troops were to hold on, the withdrawal was almost completed and by midnight the last British troops had left the summit. By dawn, the Boers had re-occupied Spion Kop. In twelve hours' fighting they had lost 60 killed, but the British casualties came to 750 men killed and wounded.

CAVALRY

In 1874 the Emperor of Russia offered a prize for the best history of cavalry. The prize of 50,000 roubles was won by Colonel George Denison, a Canadian officer, who predicted that 'mounted rifles' would be extensively used in the future, and in his book attacked the 'prejudice' amongst the professional cavalry officers against use of firearms by cavalry 'which was universal and very extensive'. The lessons of the Civil War in America and indeed of Sedan, however, went unheeded, and the few British cavalry regiments in South Africa at the beginning of the Boer War still regarded the sword and the lance as their prime weapons. Yet the war was one of movement, of surprise attacks, with the Boers mounted on their sturdy ponies, armed only with rifles sweeping in from a flank. Stopping short of a crest, or making for a fold in the ground, they would fling themselves from their ponies and open a murderous fire, often at very

169

short range. The tide only turned for the British after large reinforcements of cavalry and mounted riflemen began to arrive in South Africa. British yeomanry regiments were joined by Colonial troops and locally raised auxiliaries to bring the total of mounted troops under the leadership of the new Commander-in-Chief, Lord Kitchener, to over 175,000 men. They fought, however, as mounted riflemen, and the charge of two squadrons, from the 5th Dragoon Guards and the 5th Royal Irish Lancers, into the retreating Boers at the Battle of Elandslaagte finds a place in the history books because it was practically the only such charge in the whole of the war.

THE RUSSO-JAPANESE WAR

In the war in the Far East of 1904–5 sea power gave Japan the victory over Russia, but the fighting in Manchuria, where large armies were engaged, confirmed many of the lessons of the Boer War. The Russian base at Port Arthur was 5,500 miles from Moscow and the sole link was the Trans-Siberian Railway, so the Russians were never able to use their superior numbers and were forced to take the defensive. The Japanese Army had been trained by German officers, and to begin with used the skirmish line and column method of attack. It was not the heavy casualties, which they almost disregarded, but the fact that their frontal attacks rarely succeeded that made them adopt different tactics. Advances were made at night wherever possible and if the infantry were caught under fire by day and unable to get forward they dug in, the soldiers being taught to do this while lying on the ground. Daylight attacks were made in open order with the men creeping forward, or making short rushes in groups. The Russian soldiers had been taught that victories were won by shock action. Their infantry always had their bayonets fixed and still fired volleys, but they soon began to imitate their opponents. When

170

attacking in open country, the men ran forward in Indian file at ten-pace intervals, stooping low and using what cover they could find. As the war progressed, the artillery on both sides was forced to use indirect fire, now made much easier through the introduction of field telephones. German and British observers particularly reported on the extensive use of machine guns in defence. During the siege of Port Arthur the Russians beat off several night attacks by using searchlights alongside their Maxim guns. It was the Japanese, however, with their Hotchkiss guns, who began to use machine guns in the attack. On one occasion, six Hotchkiss guns were stealthily carried forward into a position from where they could fire at 1,500 yards' range across a river into Russian positions, half-way up a mountainside, and in a few moments they had accounted for over 1,000 Russian casualties. The Japanese also began to use overhead fire to keep the defenders' heads down during an attack. The use of quick-firing guns, machine guns, magazine rifles and barbed wire in this war greatly increased the powers of the defence. The cavalry mostly fought on foot, relying entirely on their carbines

Russo–Japanese War; a Japanese infantry attack

171

Chapter Nine

Total War and Stalemate

By the turn of the century the efforts of the European powers to avoid a major conflict had begun to break down. Bismarck's policy of forming alliances with Germany's neighbours had led to the isolation of France. But on the accession of Kaiser Wilhelm II, the Iron Chancellor had been removed and fear of the growing strength of Germany brought alliances between Britain, France and Russia. This revived Germany's fear not only of encirclement, but of a war on two fronts. The Central Powers, formed by Germany and Austro–Hungary, now made a secret treaty with Turkey, and sent a military mission to train the Turkish Army. Of all the great powers, only the United States stood apart, retaining its independence and isolationist foreign policy. In 1897, a Polish banker, Ivan Bloch, published a book forecasting that the destructive power of modern weapons would lead to 'increased slaughter on so terrible a scale as to render it impossible to get troops to push the battle to a decisive issue' and that stalemate could result, together with 'the bankruptcy of nations and the break-up of the whole social organisation'. Bloch prophesied that the war would be one of entrenchments, 'where the spade will be as indispensable to the soldier as his rifle'. Few statesmen or soldiers, however, were prepared to listen to a mere civilian who could know nothing of war. Ignoring the lessons of recent wars, many saw the introduction of quick-firing guns and machine guns, which had so dramatically increased the power of the defence, as justification for a policy of mass offensive action. Plans for the mobilisation of even larger armies were perfected, but the problems of supplying and maintaining millions of men in the field were neither understood nor seriously considered. All were agreed that if war came it would be quickly decided according to Napoleon's maxim 'that victory goes to the biggest battalions'. In one sense the Great War that opened in August, 1914, with the German invasion of Belgium—in accordance with the plan of Field Marshal Alfred von Schlieffen to sweep round and envelop the French armies that were intent on their own offensive into Lorraine—became a world war with all the great powers, including America, becoming involved. The decisive front was the Western Front in France and Belgium. It was also a total war, in that whole nations became committed, with morale on the home front as vital as that in the trenches, and battles being decided as much by the factory workers as the soldiers in the line. Man's instinct for self-preservation was now to be tested as never before and, as the vision of a quick victory faded, both sides desperately sought to develop new weapons and techniques to break the deadlock. Three recent inventions, however, were to have increasing influence on the pattern of warfare itself, and first we must bring into perspective the achievement of four men: Gottlieb Daimler, Orville and Wilbur Wright and Guglielmo Marconi.

In 1901 Marconi demonstrated to the world the enormous potential of his invention by sending wireless messages across the Atlantic between Cornwall and Newfoundland. Permanent wireless stations were soon established in many countries, and as early as 1909, foreign radio traffic was being intercepted by the

Austrian army in an attempt to break the cipher codes in use in neighbouring countries. The early transmitters were very heavy and cumbersome, and tall mast aerials had to be used. From a military point of view these early wireless sets only had a limited use in the field, but they were soon brought into use on battleships and also in fortresses. By 1914, wireless sections were found in all armies, and were principally used for sending out operation instructions in code and tapped out in Morse. Speech transmission was still in its infancy, and very few portable sets were capable of satisfactory results. Because the combined transmitting and receiving sets were still so heavy they were sited at the larger and more static headquarters, although a short-range set had been developed that could be carried in a lorry or on a horse-drawn limber for use with a cavalry division. For instance, an army head-quarters might have three heavy sets capable of trans-mitting and receiving at a range of about 150 miles and a light set for the cavalry division which had a range of about 50 miles.

By the end of the war, transportable field sets (two-man load) were operating over ranges of up to twenty

Field wireless station in 1914

miles, but the equipment was still heavy, and a tall aerial had to be erected every time the station was set up.

The invention of the petrol engine by Gottlieb Daimler had come much earlier, in 1882. Before the turn of the century the French Army had experimented on manœuvres with the use of motor vehicles and Count Ferdinand von Zeppelin's airship, which was 400 feet long and fitted with two propellers driven by tiny petrol engines, had made its first halting flight. The first motorcycle was produced in 1901, and two years later the Wright brothers became the first men to fly (if only for twelve seconds) in a petrol-engined aeroplane. The age of oil had come, bringing a third dimension to warfare.

AIRSHIPS

Count Zeppelin's airship was designed as a series of individual compartments filled with hydrogen—each in effect a balloon—encased in a rigid framework of light metal girders and covered with fabric. One or more gondolas carrying the engines and crew were slung below the airship. In 1908, Count Zeppelin made a flight of twenty-four hours in an airship 446 feet long and 42 feet in diameter. The German Government

A Zeppelin – note the spy car being lowered

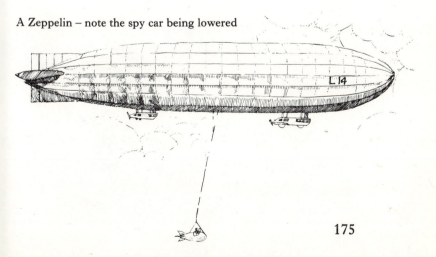

now began to pour money into the production of rigid airships, and by 1912, over 1,600 passenger flights had been made without serious incident. Germany entered the war with only six military versions of the Zeppelin, but immediately launched a massive construction programme. In all, sixty-one airships were commissioned, but only ten survived the war; the remainder were shot down or lost in bad weather on hazardous missions. At the outbreak of war, Germany lost several airships on reconnaissance flights because they flew too low, presenting an easy target for gun and small-arms fire. The very first air raid was made by a Zeppelin which early in August, 1914, dropped a number of artillery shells on the Belgian town of Liège, but the Zeppelin was hit by gun fire and crashed in a forest near Bonn. By September, the Germans had produced small aerial bombs and 2,000 pounds' weight of these were dropped on Antwerp. Both of these raids were made by night, but no military targets were hit. The effect, however, on the civilian population, of these aerial monsters roaming at will over almost defenceless cities was very great. Starting in January

3-inch anti-aircraft
gun

of the following year, the Zeppelins were sent across the North Sea to bomb the British towns and cities. The first raid on London was in May, 1915, by which time small incendiary bombs were added to the high explosive bombs and even hand grenades were used in the attacks. At this time, the defences of London consisted of twelve guns, only two of which were of 3-inch calibre, and twelve small searchlights. As the anti-aircraft defences improved and the aeroplane was developed, the Zeppelins were forced to fly higher and higher. Eventually in clear weather they were operating at the astonishing altitude of 25,000 feet, at which height the crew had to use oxygen and suffered terribly from the intense cold. Zeppelins now took to flying above, or even in, thick clouds, and were very difficult to detect, as the sound of the engines was muffled. As a Zeppelin neared its target, an observer would be lowered, perhaps several thousand feet in a basket, or 'spy car', to just below the base of the clouds. Using compass bearings and a telephone connected to the cable, the lone observer would then manœuvre the airship over the target, and the bombs would rain down as if from an empty sky.

AIRCRAFT

In the two years immediately prior to the outbreak of war, France held all the world records for aircraft performance. The British, however, had produced, at what later became the Royal Aircraft Establishment at Farnborough, the first truly stable and manœuvrable aircraft, while Germany, previously mesmerised by her success with airships, suddenly realised the importance of the aeroplane and opened a military flying school. In France, a Deperdussin racing monoplane with a 160-horse-power Gnome engine had flown at 126 miles per hour, and the endurance and height records were 634 miles and 20,000 feet. The BE2 biplane, built at

177

B E 2 Reconnaissance aircraft

Farnborough, proved to be the most successful of the early reconnaissance machines and nearly 2,000 were subsequently brought into service. For manœuvrability and rate of climb, however, the Sopwith Tabloid, which first flew at Farnborough in 1913, was outstanding. The Tabloid, with an 80-horse-power Gnome engine had a top speed of ninety-two miles per hour, and could climb to 15,000 feet in ten minutes. Fitted with floats, it won the second Schneider trophy race for seaplanes at double the average speed put up by the French.

When war broke out, the approximate number of military aircraft sent to the Western Front was 65 British, 155 French and 260 German. Most of these aircraft could only fly at a maximum speed of about seventy-five miles per hour, and none was designed for air-to-air fighting. Their role was reconnaissance and until radios were fitted, late in 1917, the pilots had to drop their messages on a headquarters, or fly back to their landing grounds to make their report. When trench warfare started, aerial photography became very important as all kinds of details about the defences were disclosed by the camera. Day after day, pilots were sent out over the enemy's line. The cameras were heavy and clumsy, and the slow, two-seater aircraft, flying

178

'straight and level' even for the short time it needed to make the exposures, presented a fine target to the anti-aircraft gunners. Back at the landing ground, intelligence officers were waiting to examine the prints. Belts of barbed wire and trench systems showed up as clearly as roads and rivers on an ordinary printed map. The art of camouflage suddenly became vitally important. A heavy gun painted a dull, neutral colour and covered with a few branches might avoid detection by a pilot flying his flimsy machine in the face of heavy anti-aircraft fire, but the camera saw the tracks made by the gun moving into position and the heavy shadows cast by the gun itself, unless this was carefully disguised by netting and canvas strips. Similarly, the position of a headquarters could be given away by signallers taking a short cut across the corner of a field and leaving a tell-tale track. As soon as lightweight radio sets were available, many of the slow, two-seater aircraft were given the role of becoming the eyes of the artillery, spotting targets and transmitting corrections to the batteries firing below. The BE2 was typical of these early two-seater reconnaissance aircraft. It had an endurance of about three and a half hours, took forty-five minutes to climb to 10,000 feet, and had a maximum speed of 75 miles per hour.

With both sides constantly flying over enemy territory it was not long before the airmen started their own individual war, taking pot shots at each other with revolver or rifle, and later with machine guns fired sideways from the cockpit. The British had already developed a two-seater pusher biplane with the engine and propeller behind the wings to thrust the aircraft forward. This was the Vickers FB5, known as the Gunbus, which was now put into production. The observer sat right out in the front of the nascelle, where he had a wide arc of fire, operating a machine gun mounted on a pedestal. Although the Gunbus was too slow to catch the German single-seater Scout aircraft,

A 'Gunbus' fighter aircraft

it gave the Allies a decided advantage during the summer of 1915. Meanwhile, Anthony Fokker, a Dutch designer working for the Germans, had invented a means of controlling the fire of a forward-mounted machine gun by an interrupter gear so that the bullets passed between the propeller blades. This invention revolutionised air fighting. By the winter of 1915, Fokker's Eindecker monoplane fighter with its synchronised gun was dominating the skies over the Western Front. The 'Fokker scourge' lasted for nearly nine months before the Allies were able to produce a comparable fighter aircraft.

KITE BALLOONS

The kite balloon was a German invention. It was shaped like a sausage and had a tail consisting of a large bag which filled with air and acted as a rudder, keeping the balloon steady and head on to the wind. Balloons were used for artillery spotting and local reconnaissance, and at sea for watching out for submarines and directing gun fire. Having copied the German *drachen* (kite) design, the Allies began to use observation balloons on the Western Front in 1915. Curiously enough, aircraft found the balloons rather difficult to destroy. Attacks with incendiary bullets had to be made at a range of fifty yards or less, and in wet

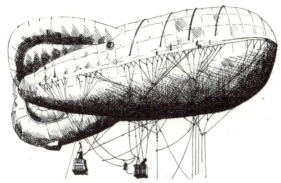

Kite observation balloon

weather it was almost impossible to set fire to a balloon. Observation balloons were tethered by a steel cable to a winch driven by a steam engine. Later, a petrol engine was used which was capable of hauling down a balloon at 1,200 feet per minute. To begin with, balloons could only be flown up to 2,000 feet when the wind speed was less than twenty-eight miles per hour, but by the end of the war, balloons were flying at 7,000 feet and in winds of up to sixty miles per hour. Very large kite balloons were produced for the defences of London, supporting an apron of steel cables, at a height of up to 15,000 feet to make it difficult for the German raiders to fly in at low altitude.

MOBILISATION—MEN AND SUPPLIES

Faced with a war on two fronts, Germany had planned for a quick victory in the West before turning on the Russians. Under the direction of their General Staff the Germans had expanded their railway system and brought it to such a high pitch of efficiency that on mobilisation over 3 million men, carried in 11,000 trains, were moved to the Western Front in eleven days. Every day, 550 trains crossed the Rhine bridges, and at the Hohenzollern Bridge at Cologne, a train crossed every ten minutes day and night. On the Continent conscription was the rule; Austria on the one side and France and Russia on the other, all mobilised over 2 million men. Britain, who only introduced conscription in 1916, sent an expeditionary force of five divisions, totalling 160,000 men, which took up its position on the left of the French Army near the Belgian frontier. The British Expeditionary Force, long-term regulars to a man, was very small compared with other Continental armies, but the most highly trained in the world, and aptly described by the late Sir Basil Liddell Hart as, 'a rapier amongst scythes'. As the war dragged on, the size of the armies grew. Britain mobilised 5 million in her armed forces, and the United States nearly as many. By the end of the war, 65 million men of all nations had borne arms.

Once the troops had left the train that had rushed them to the frontier, the rate of advance of the army was that of the marching infantry, but only so long as ammunition and supplies could be carried forward from the nearest 'railhead'. For the units within the division horse transport was universal. Guns, limbers, supply wagons and ambulances were all horse-drawn. Staff cars and dispatch riders on motorcycles soon became a familiar sight near the large headquarters,

Horse transport on the march

but to begin with there were few motor lorries for carrying supplies, and the only motor ambulances sent to the front came from voluntary organisations. The supply lorries in any case were fitted with solid tyres and incapable of moving across country. The difficulties of supplying the huge armies in the early

Supply lorries in France

months of the war were enormous and had never been fully appreciated before. Within three months the Allies in France had managed to collect nearly 20,000 motor vehicles to operate between the ports and railheads and the fighting troops. But when stalemate came, the demands for ammunition and engineering stores of all kinds rose to astronomical proportions and the dependence of the armies on motor transport grew year by year until the number of motor vehicles needed to keep the troops supplied had multiplied ten times. Both in the air and on land, the petrol engine had begun to shape the future pattern of war.

MONS AND LE CATEAU

While the Germans were sweeping down through Belgium, the French launched an offensive towards Metz, but were repulsed with a loss of 140,000 men in four days. On the left of the French armies the British Expeditionary Force had advanced as far as Mons, and units began to take up entrenched positions along the canal and covering the town to the east. When the French withdrew they found themselves isolated and under attack by the German First Army. The battle of Mons lasted for nine hours and the whole weight of the German attack fell on two British divisions. The Germans appeared to be attacking in mass formation as line upon line of infantry in field-grey uniforms advanced

183

almost shoulder to shoulder. Trained to fire fifteen aimed shots a minute, the British broke up several attacks at 800 yards, even while the Germans were forming up. Subsequent attacks opened with a long and heavy artillery bombardment, but when the German infantry rushed forward they were simply mown down and many of the German officers were convinced that the British had a large number of machine guns. In fact, the British battalions at this time only had two old-pattern Maxim guns. Six German divisions were thrown into the attack and their casualties have never been disclosed. The British, however, held their positions for twenty-four hours with the loss of 1,600 men. The standard of musketry training in the British army in 1914 was very high, and a third-class shot who showed no sign of improvement was liable to be discharged for inefficiency. The record for rapid fire with the SMLE rifle dates from this period—thirty-eight rounds in one minute, all within the inner ring of a man-sized target at 300 yards.

Three days later the Germans faced the same British corps near the little town of Le Cateau. The British had been without rations for three days and, exhausted by continuous marching in the intense heat, had turned to fight because the infantry could march no further. A series of low ridges gave a field of fire and some cover for the gunners and the infantry had dug in where they had halted. On the right, the artillery commander chose to site his guns for direct fire, sending them forward close behind the infantry. On the remainder of the frontage, batteries were given carefully concealed positions and dug in. Firing shrapnel, the British field guns broke up the German attacks time and time again. The exposed guns on the right, however, soon became the target for salvoes of ninety-pound high explosive shells from the German 150-mm. heavy howitzers and suffered terrible casualties. When time came to withdraw, twenty-six out of forty-two guns that had been firing over open sights from exposed positions had to be abandoned. The remainder were only withdrawn with extreme difficulty and crippling losses in men and horses. The guns in the other sector, however, had very few casualties. Using indirect fire from concealed positions they continued to support the infantry all day, doing tremendous execution. When the withdrawal was ordered they moved quietly off, unseen by the Germans. After Le Cateau there could be no longer any doubt of the value of indirect fire from concealed positions, as the Boers had shown years before. The very fact that the guns were sited further back also enabled them to fire on a wider arc without having to move. This in turn brought a greater concentration of fire as several batteries could engage the same target.

ARTILLERY

Having carefully studied the lessons of the Russo–Japanese War, the Germans were not only better trained in the use of machine guns but had concentrated on developing heavy howitzers. A number of 5·9- and 8-inch howitzers were included in each German division.

German heavy howitzer

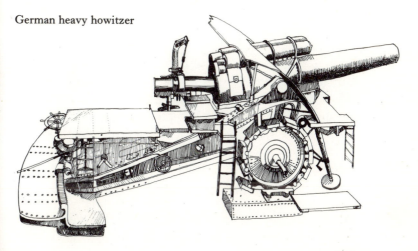

At the outbreak of war the British had more field guns and some field howitzers, but only four 60-pounder guns as heavy artillery with each division. The French 75, with a maximum range of 7,440 yards, was still the best in the world, although the German field gun could outrange it by nearly 2,000 yards. The British field artillery consisted of 18- and 13-pounder field guns and 4·5-inch howitzers, all with a maximum range of 7,000 yards. The new field guns embodied the Armstrong wire-wound barrel and the Vickers recoil system, and they fired shrapnel. In 1914, armies marched into battle without any kind of anti-aircraft defence. In Germany, the firms of Krupp and Erhardt had designed a wide range of guns for use against airships, but the problems of hitting the small and more elusive aeroplane had

British field gun in action

seemed quite unsurmountable. Field-gun equipment such as the French 75 and the British 13-pounder were quickly adapted to fire from heavy pedestal mountings. The British 3-inch anti-aircraft gun, which on its mountings weighed 2,240 pounds, is typical of the new kind of gun that was now needed in large quantities for defence against the rapidly growing menace of air attack.

The German plans to sweep down and envelop Paris had failed and so had the French counter-offensive. At the height of the Battle of the Marne a complete French division was rushed to the front by 600 Paris

A Paris taxi in 1914

taxi cabs—the first mass use of motor vehicles in war. This was an isolated incident and the ebb and flow of battle was still at the pace of the marching infantry. There were no sweeping cavalry charges, no dramatic attacks by massed infantry rushing forward with the bayonet, as the French had attempted in the first few weeks of the war. In the face of the tremendous fire power of modern artillery and machine guns, neither side could succeed in breaking through and deadlock resulted. What had started as a war of movement, that would be 'over by Christmas', now became a vast siege operation. The narrow strip of 'no man's land' between the entrenched armies was now dominated by the very weapons that had brought stalemate.

TRENCH WARFARE

In spite of the lessons of recent wars, the need for infantry in defence to 'dig in' was generally regarded as an almost retrograde step which merely marked a temporary phase in mobile operations. On pre-war manœuvres trench digging was unpopular as the troops had to go back and fill them in at the end of the day. Training manuals gave elaborate details for the construction of field fortifications, but the necessary engineering stores just did not exist, and no army had thought it necessary to study the question of special weapons and equipment needed for static warfare. When their

187

A trench scene

initial plans went awry the German High Command attempted to outflank the Allies by attacking towards the Channel ports, in what became known as 'the race to the sea'. In the other sectors they took up good defensive positions which could be held by fewer troops, so as to release more divisions for their new offensive. In the Battle of Ypres, they again failed to break through and, having had to divert troops to the Russian Front, the Germans were on the defensive by the end of November, 1914, along the whole of the Western Front. Both sides had suffered terrible casualties, and the exhausted troops now faced each other along a front that stretched for 475 miles, from the Swiss border to the North Sea east of Dunkirk. The shallow 'shelter' trenches, hastily sited along a ditch or road embankment, or perhaps in the open, where there was a good field of fire, and scratched out with entrenching tools might offer protection from small-arms fire, but became a death trap when the enemy guns opened up. Concealment was impossible, and the Germans with their numerous observation balloons had the advantage. Men's lives now depended on the spade and pickaxe, as the shallow trenches were deepened and traverses dug at an angle to localise the effect of a direct hit. As a continuous line was formed, trench stores became as vital as ammunition—millions of sandbags to build the parapets and fire steps, wattle fencing, wooden planks, more sandbags, anything that would shore up the steep sides of the deepening trenches. Much of the Allied line had to be built in low-lying country, with water a few feet below the surface. Here men fought and died up to their waists in water. The enemy artillery, 2,000 yards behind their own front line, could stop the bringing forward of supplies by day, but at night tracks and crossroads became targets for harassing fire. Everything had to go below ground. Communication trenches zig-zagged towards the rear, so that reliefs and supplies could be brought up; telephone lines had to be buried; a support and reserve line of trenches had to be dug further to the rear to guard against a breakthrough. In the dry sectors it was possible to construct dugouts for shelter against the weather and anything but a direct hit. Here were to be found the command posts, with the signallers, the

A headquarters dug-out

'No man's land'

medical orderlies, the runners who carried messages if
the telephone lines were cut by shell fire, and the men
who had been working all night repairing the barbed-
wire fences or rebuilding a trench that had been cratered
by the direct hit of a high explosive shell. The front
line on both sides was covered by two belts of barbed-
wire entanglement, each about ten yards thick, and
some ten to twenty yards apart, so sited that an enemy
attack checked on the wire would be enfiladed by
machine gun and rifle fire from several points of the
zig-zag front trench line. On an average, the two front
lines were about 200 or 300 yards apart, but in places,
and in particular in the British sectors, they were often
as near as 25 yards from each other. Under such conditions the fighting often became a kind of duel between
men armed with hand grenades, clubs, knives and even
sharpened shovels. In the narrow strip of 'no man's
land', a landscape pock-marked with shell holes and
scarred with twisted wire and shattered tree stumps, a
leafless copse, or a pile of mouldering rubble where

Stick grenade and Mills hand grenade

German rifle
grenade

190

a house had stood, became the arena in which men crouched and crawled and listened, a place of ambush and the sudden raid to snatch a sentry or destroy a machine-gun nest. A place of death and desolation which could suddenly erupt with the crash of shell fire and the chatter of the machine gun as the bullets whipped across the tortured ground. Stick grenades and improved patterns of the cricket-ball type, like the Mills bomb, were put into urgent production to replace the jam tins filled with explosive that were improvised locally. Periscopes, wire cutters, hand torches and pocket compasses now became an essential issue and always seemed to be in short supply.

THE LEWIS GUN

The machine gun now held a dominant place. The Germans had started the war with over 12,500 Maxims and now introduced a light pattern weighing thirty-four pounds with a tripod mount and a drum-shaped magazine which could be used by one man. Shortly before the war Isaac Lewis, an American artillery officer, had perfected a light gas-operated machine gun which in 1912 had been the first machine gun to be fired from an aircraft. The Lewis gun had a unique cooling system—an aluminium 'radiator' with seventeen broad flanges fitted over the barrel—and both were enclosed in a light steel casing. The casing was tapered at the muzzle end and when the gun was fired the muzzle blast created a vacuum which drew in cold air from the rear to cool the barrel and prevent overheating. The magazine held forty-seven rounds and

Lewis gun

191

weighed four pounds. It fitted on top of the gun which itself only weighed twenty-five pounds. Using a sling, one man could fire the Lewis gun on the move, but it was normally fired off the small bipod mount which was only a foot high. In almost any landscape a Lewis gun was practically invisible at 400 yards. The gun was fired in short bursts of five to twenty rounds, and could keep up a steady rate of fire which was the equivalent of the rifle fire of fifty men. The production of Lewis guns was started before the war by the Birmingham Small Arms Company. They were first issued in 1915 on the scale of two per battalion to replace the Vickers machine guns that were brigaded in the newly

Vickers Medium
Machine Gun

formed Machine Gun Corps. By 1918, every British battalion had no fewer than thirty-six Lewis guns, and this remarkable and revolutionary weapon had been extensively used by both the British and American air forces. Firing incendiary bullets, the Lewis gun was officially credited with destroying ten out of the twelve Zeppelins that were shot down over London.

GAS WARFARE

The Germans were quick to realise the prohibitive cost of attacks against entrenched infantry supported by machine guns and massed artillery, and they eagerly sought new weapons to break the stranglehold of trench warfare. Early in 1915, they used shells filled with tear gas against the Russians on the Eastern Front near

Warsaw, but the attack was a costly failure as the drops of liquid failed to evaporate in the intense cold. An alternative method of employing gas, however, was suggested by a certain Sergeant Haver. Fritz Haver, a scientist with an international reputation, was little known in his own country. Like many thousands of German Jews he had volunteered at the outbreak of war to serve in the army. By a quirk of fate, Haver—who later received a Nobel Prize for the synthetic production of ammonia, a discovery of enormous value to agriculture—achieved far greater notoriety as the 'inventor of gas warfare'. Germany had a highly developed chemical industry and his plan was easy to implement, although Captain Haver, as he had now become, took pains to warn the German Generals of the terrible retribution that could result from a general adoption of gas warfare, unless they achieved a quick victory, as the Allies had access to far greater quantities of raw materials. Large quantities of cylinders filled with liquid chlorine were assembled in the German front-line trenches opposite the Allied salient of Ypres. When the wind was favourable a yellow cloud of poison gas would be released to billow and swirl over the enemy's lines, filling every trench and dugout and hole in the ground to bring convulsions, stupor and a choking death to the luckless defenders. The Germans

First German
gas mask

British gas helmet

opposite Ypres had to wait fourteen days before the wind conditions were right. In spite of reports from prisoners and even from their own pilots and patrols, who had actually seen the cylinders dug in close to the German trenches, the gas attack came as a complete surprise to the Allies. Within a matter of hours there was a five-mile gap in the Allied line where two French divisions had suffered the terrible effects of the initial gas attack, but as darkness fell the Germans were seen digging in, and their opportunity for a clean break-through faded. Allied reinforcements were rushed forward, and after desperate fighting that lasted a whole month, and cost over 100,000 casualties to both sides, the breach in the Allied lines was eventually sealed.

Front-line troops hated gas and everything to do with it and if the decision had been left to the fighting soldiers it would never have been used. The gas mask first issued to the Germans was a very elementary and clumsy affair, a pad of tow soaked in chemicals and tied over the mouth and nose. Later, a metal nose-clip was added, and it became known as the 'snout'. It is strange that the German General Staff had not bothered to ask their meteorologists, or even some of their pilots, about the prevailing winds on the Western Front. These favoured the Allies nine days out of ten, so it was not long before the Germans had a taste of their own medicine from cloud gas being blown back over their own line when the wind suddenly veered round. The Allies had to improvise masks from what they could requisition locally. Pads of black veiling or flannel were

German gas shell

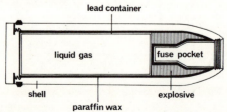

194

made up ready to be dipped in buckets of chemicals kept ready in the front line. Red Cross workers in England made as many as a million pads of cotton wool and gauze in a single day. Unfortunately these proved useless as air would not pass through the cotton wool after it had been wetted.

The introduction of gas shells filled with new and extremely lethal gases such as phosgene brought an entirely new problem, as many troops within artillery range could be subjected to gas attack without warning by day or night. Hoods or helmets made of flannel, treated with chemicals and kept moist with glycerine, were now issued. These fitted right over the head and tucked into the neck of the tunic. Celluloid eye pieces cracked easily and were replaced by glass. Later, a tube and valve for breathing out was fitted to the mask, to prevent carbon dioxide accumulating from the user's breath. Finally, 'box' respirators were issued. These fitted close round the face and could be worn with reasonable comfort for quite long periods. The air was drawn in through a mouthpiece and valve after passing through a metal canister or box filled with chemicals.

Mustard gas, which had the most terrible and long-lasting effects, was introduced by the Germans in 1917. Smelling like garlic, a drop of this persistent, oily liquid was disabling if it came in contact with the skin, or produced permanent blindness from momentary exposure without a satisfactory mask. Mustard gas was particularly dangerous because ground, or even clothing, contaminated with the liquid gave off poisonous vapour for as long as ten days, especially in cold weather, after the gas attack had been launched. As Haver had forecast, the Allies in the last two years of the war were able to produce gas shells and canisters in far greater quantities than the Germans. The total casualties from the use of poison gas by both sides amounted to nearly 2 million. But for the constant vigilance of the scientists in detecting new kinds of gas, and the enforcement of rigid discipline over the wearing of masks and carrying out decontamination precautions, many more men would have died or suffered life-long disablement.

FLAMETHROWERS

Flamethrowers were introduced by the Germans in June, 1915. Some were of the portable or 'pack' type carried on the back, rather like the spray equipment sometimes used for fruit trees. Their range was only twenty yards or less, but the sudden jet of burning oil which produced intense heat and a cloud of black smoke had considerable psychological effect. The problem, however, was to get close enough for this potentially terrifying weapon to be effective. Allied machine gunners, with their Lewis or Hotchkiss guns, usually succeeded in wiping out a 'flame' attack by concentrating on those men who were obviously struggling forward under a heavy load. The largest flamethrower used during the war was designed by a British scientist, George Livens. The apparatus was heavy and cumbersome, but had a range of nearly 100 yards. The various parts were made so that they could be carried into the front line as a two-man load, but altogether the equivalent of 2–300 men had to make the trip before everything needed was assembled. It was usually necessary to dig a mine shaft towards the enemy's lines so that the flamethrower could be assembled in one of the galleries (some ten to fifteen feet below the surface) within range of the German trenches. At the last moment before the attack, the heads of the two jets would be pushed up so as to stick out about two feet above the ground. A few seconds afterwards, when the signal for the attack was given, automatic lighters would fire the oil which shot out under enormous pressure supplied by gas cylinders. As the jets slowly traversed from side to side, a ton of flaming oil swept towards the German trenches with a roar, 'while dense clouds of black smoke flecked with flame rose a hundred feet into the air'. Although highly successful on several occasions, the equipment was far too heavy and complicated to be generally used.

THE LIVENS PROJECTOR

Livens now turned to a type of projector that was more mobile and had a far greater range—this was simply a *fougasse*, or mortar, which he improvised from steel tubing, to hurl bombs into the enemy's position at a range of up to a mile. The projectors, looking exactly like drain pipes, were dug in and camouflaged in batteries of about twenty-five. The propellant charge in the base of the projector was fired by electricity and all the bombs in any battery were usually fired simultaneously. On one occasion, nearly 4,000 projectors were discharged in a single operation. This versatile, but somewhat inaccurate, weapon fired almost anything —gas-filled bombs containing thirty pounds of phosgene, cylinders containing high explosive or oil which would burst into flames on contact, and even harmless substances such as amyl acetate which simulated gas to make the enemy put on their gas masks at the moment of an infantry assault. By comparison, the German 18-cm. *minenwerfer* had very much smaller bombs containing about sixteen pounds of gas, which were known as 'rum jars'.

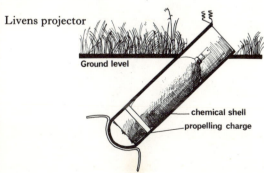

Livens projector

Ground level

chemical shell
propelling charge

TRENCH MORTARS

There is nothing new in the idea of using a comparatively small charge to hurl a projectile high into the air to reach an enemy that is nearby but sheltered from direct fire, and ever since the invention of gunpowder the mortar has played its part in siege warfare. Before the war the Germans laid in stocks of *minenwerfer* (literally bomb throwers) which, like their heavy machine guns, were used as infantry-support weapons and now became trench artillery. The French had to make do with old bronze siege mortars and the British had none at all—a situation that both armies were quick to remedy just as soon as production could be started. The trench mortar had many advantages over the conventional gun or howitzer. It was simple and cheap to manufacture and used smaller propellant charges. It was considerably lighter and could be taken to pieces and set up in a confined space and moved from one emplacement to another. With a high trajectory, it was ideal for lobbing shells into the enemy's trenches or into dead ground, and it could fire with safety much closer to one's own troops than a gun or even a howitzer. For instance, the 7·6-cm. *minenwerfer* which weighed 312 pounds was less than an eighth of the weight of a field gun of the same calibre and still had a range of 1,400 yards. The 24·5-cm. heavy *minenwerfer*, however, was a much more solid affair which weighed 1,963

Minenwerfer –
light model (76 mm)

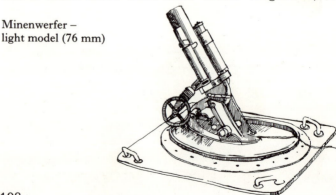

198

pounds and needed twenty-one men to bring it into action. Yet it fired a shell of the same size as that of a heavy gun which was relatively immobile and extremely difficult to conceal. These German mortars were rifled, muzzle-loading and had recoil mechanism, and they could be easily moved by road or across firm ground on the two wheels which fitted on to either side of the

Minenwerfer on flat trajectory carriage

base plate. Early in 1917, the light *minenwerfer* (7·6-cm. calibre) was modified and a broad, concave spade added to the base plate so that it could fire with a flat trajectory like a field gun off the ground (elevation from 0° to 38°) or in a mobile role with the wheels on (elevation from 8° to 54°).

THE STOKES MORTAR

By midsummer 1915, the Allies were critically short of gun ammunition so when quantities of trench mortars were needed urgently it was very important that the type adopted, as well as the necessary ammunition, should be capable of speedy manufacture by firms not already fully committed to armament supply. A single, daring invention, at first considered impracticable and

199

even dangerous, turned out to be one of the outstanding successes of the war. This was the Stokes Light Mortar. The prototype consisted simply of a steel tube; the sealed end contained the firing pin and rested on a base plate dug into the ground at an angle; the fore-end was supported on a light bipod frame with an elevating screw. The bomb, weighing fifteen pounds, fitted the barrel loosely and had an ordinary 12-bore sporting cartridge slipped into its base. When the bomb

Stokes Mortar (3 inch)

was dropped down the barrel, the cartridge was exploded by the spike at the bottom of the barrel and the whole projectile hurled to a range of up to 350 yards. The bursting fuse on the bomb was initially ignited by the explosion of the cartridge. The range was adjusted by using a clinometer to set the barrel at different angles. This original model was rejected as unsafe by military experts but fortunately Lloyd George, the British Prime Minister, saw it demonstrated and promptly ordered 1,000 to be manufactured and urgent experimental work to start on an improved fuse for the bomb. By September, an order had been placed for an initial supply of 100,000 of the new type of bombs. The Stokes mortar was so simple in design that it could be turned out by almost any small engineering firm. It was also easy to operate and a well-trained crew

200

could load so rapidly that no less than fifteen bombs could be seen in the air before the first one struck the target. The 3-inch Stokes mortar firing high explosive eventually became a standard infantry weapon for the Allies and the 4-inch model was extensively used for gas warfare, as the bomb held four times as much liquid gas as a 6-inch howitzer shell. Improvements included the use of cordite propellant charges to increase the range to 1,600 yards and an 'anvil' type exploder in the base of the bomb, as it was found the fixed firing pin quickly wore out. Finally, an 'all ways' percussion fuse was produced which exploded the bomb whichever way it fell the instant it struck the ground. As the bomb flew through the air, a tiny safety bar was pulled out by a spring-loaded tape so that on impact a lead ball and striker fired the flash powder, which connected to an instantaneous fuse. The popularity of the Stokes mortars was such that in February, 1916, a further order for 2,400 of the 3-inch mortars and ammunition at the rate of 176,000 rounds a week was given. By the end of the war, nearly 12 million rounds of standard 3-inch bombs had been supplied by the 'little firms' dotted all over the British Isles.

German grenade thrower used in trench warfare

Chapter Ten

The Return of Armour

The Generals on both sides eventually realised that attacks against entrenched positions, which were covered by machine guns and protected by deep wire entanglements, invariably failed with terrible loss. The use of gas had proved indecisive, and the only solution seemed to be more and more guns to blast a way through. In 1915, the Germans were manufacturing 250,000 rounds of gun ammunition a day, twice as much as the French, and ten times as much as the British. In the opening day of the Battle of Neuve Chapelle, the first serious attempt at an Allied breakthrough, the British fired more shells than in the whole of the South African War. The bombardment on a 2,000-yard front lasted thirty-five minutes and much of the German front line was captured. The attack, however, was halted on a ridge farther back by German counter-attacks. The failure, which was largely due to a breakdown of communications between the infantry and the gunners struggling to move forward over the broken ground, was attributed to a shortage of ammunition.

The French, with larger stocks of ammunition, now tried different tactics. In theory, 150 rounds from their 75-mm. field gun would cut a twelve-foot gap in a deep belt of wire, but to cut sufficient gaps and destroy the known machine-gun posts on a wide front took time, and all surprise was lost. The Germans, realising that a prolonged bombardment would destroy their trenches, merely dug deeper and deeper shelters. In the Battle of the Somme, where the bombardment lasted for seven days, the survival of a single machine gun and its crew was sufficient to wipe out a complete battalion, caught in the line formation that was considered necessary to control the assault over the shell-pocked battlefield. Shrapnel had proved useless against deep entrenchments. Commenting on the value of high explosive shells, Brigadier Shelford Bidwell wrote in *Gunners at War*, 'The landscapes of shell-craters full of liquid mud in which a man or mule could drown are evidence of its ineffectiveness, except to throw up a barrier for the attackers.' The Battle of the Somme lasted for four and a half months, and finished as a battle of attrition with the loss to both sides of over 600,000 men. With each new offensive, more and more guns were used until they stood wheel to wheel along many miles of front. First, the heavy batteries would start a gun-to-gun duel; then, after a prolonged bombardment the infantry, so heavily laden that they could only advance at a walk, would move forward in a

Eindeker Fokker fighter aircraft

succession of lines. Stumbling forward at the best pace they could make, the leading troops kept as close as possible to the creeping barrage. This was a belt of bursting shells which 'jumped' forward a hundred yards every three to four minutes. Everything depended upon the infantry capturing successive objectives according to an exact timetable based on the artillery fire plan. If anything went wrong there was no second chance; when the barrage stopped the exhausted men faced yet another line of machine guns, and with their own artillery struggling to move forward through a sea of mud to cross the shattered trenches, they were at the mercy of the German counter-attacks.

VERDUN

The city of Verdun, originally fortified by Vauban to block the valley of the Meuse, stood within a salient with the Germans on three sides. The defences had been progressively strengthened since the war of 1870–71 by a ring of armoured forts, and the more recently constructed trench systems. Believing the forts themselves could be neutralised by the German heavy howitzers, the French had ill-advisedly removed many of the fortress guns for use in the field elsewhere, but they still regarded the Verdun salient as impregnable. Convinced that France would never yield Verdun, Erich von Falkenhayn, the German Commander-in-Chief, decided to attack the salient to 'bleed her to death' in a purely symbolic struggle. The plan was to attack on a narrow front with overwhelming artillery support and, in mid-February, 1916, the Germans assembled in great secrecy six divisions, which was more than twice the strength of the defence, 1,700 guns and 2·5 million shells. The initial attack broke through the first two defence lines to a depth of four miles, and by a *coup de main* a German patrol of only ten men captured Fort Douaumont. The French, however, fought with utter disregard of the odds against them, and Marshal Henri Pétain's exhortation, *Ils ne passeront pas*, has become historic. Reinforcements began to pour down the only open road, and by the seventh day the assault had been halted. A terrible battle of attrition now followed, and bitter fighting continued for a further ten months. Along the fifty miles of narrow second-class road from Bar-le-Duc to Verdun, soon to be known as *la voie sacrée*, two-thirds of the whole French army were to pass. During the crisis of the German gas attack in June, 12,000 lorries were on the route, with one passing every fourteen seconds. Many of the soldiers bound for the inferno beyond the city never returned. The French losses, which were marginally greater than those of the Germans, amounted to 362,000 men. Day and night the shelling continued until nearly 4 million shells had fallen on the few square miles of battlefield that remains a wilderness to this day.

At Verdun, the seed was sown of the wave of discontent and despair that swept through the French Army in 1917 when many soldiers from fifty-four divisions were involved in mutinies. But in *Death of a Generation* Alistair Horne writes, 'The spirit of the German Army was never the same after 1916. Verdun and the Somme had bitten into its soul'. These two battles were indeed a turning point, but the strength of the Allies had also been sapped, and after the German withdrawal to the Hindenburg Line in March, 1917, although the Allied offensives continued with the British bearing the brunt of the fighting, there was no decision —only terrible losses in continued battles of attrition.

AMERICA ENTERS THE WAR

In April, 1917, the United States entered the war, and the first contingent of 'doughboys' arrived in France at the end of June. When the German counter-offensive opened in March, 1918, there were at least eight American divisions on the Western Front, with reinforcements constantly arriving to make up a total, by the date of the Armistice, of no less than forty-two divisions. The Americans' divisions were twice as strong as those of their Allies, and their contribution amounted to no less than 1·5 million men. There is little doubt that the arrival of the United States divisions gradually turned the tide and compensated for the diminishing effort of the French over the last eighteen months of the war.

By the autumn of 1918, the whole pattern of operations on the Western Front had changed. On the Somme, two years previously, an advance of eight miles on a twelve-mile front had involved four and a half months of fighting and an appalling number of casualties. Now, in six weeks' fighting and with less than a third of the earlier casualties, the British armies had made an average advance of twenty-five miles on a forty-mile frontage. This was the period when fourteen German divisions were driven out of the Saint-Mihiel salient by the American First Army. The attack was launched very early in the morning, in dense fog, and was supported by over 3,000 guns and air forces consisting of 1,400 aircraft, which included the British Independent Bomber Force, and 600 machines lent by the French, together with 260 light tanks. Within thirty-six hours, and at the cost of only 7,000 casualties, the Germans were driven clean out of their last remaining salient with the loss of 15,000 prisoners alone and 450 guns.

STEEL HELMETS

American infantryman in full equipment

Within weeks of the outbreak of war, many French cavalry units found themselves in the trenches. The dragoons and the cuirassiers (who had gone to war in breast-plates) still wore a huge, crested brass helmet

French steel helmets

with visor and neckpiece and a horse's tail sweeping from the back. Under the conditions of trench warfare the number of head wounds increased to alarming proportions, but it was soon noticed that the helmet gave a measure of protection from shell splinters and shrapnel. As a temporary expediency a steel skull-cap was issued to the infantry to wear inside the *képi*, but this gave no protection to the back of the neck. Towards the end of 1915, the French Army was issued with a steel helmet shaped exactly like the brass helmet worn by Paris firemen. The wide-brimmed, British 'tin hat', which was also adopted by the Americans was in general use by the middle of 1916. The German steel helmet which replaced the *pickel haube*, or spiked helmet, followed much more closely the medieval 'pudding basin' design.

ARMOURED CARS

Ever since the introduction of horse-drawn war chariots 3,000 years ago, man's inventiveness has struggled to resolve the equation: Mobility × Protection × Weapon Power. The knight in armour had to bow to the musketeer. The age of steam brought armoured trains

German steel
helmet

British steel
helmet

in the American Civil War, and an armoured road locomotive that pulled armour-plated wagons in the South African War, but neither could move off the railway tracks or roads. The rise of the machine gun coincided with the invention of the petrol engine, and immediate attempts were made to marry the newly discovered mobility and fire power. By the turn of the century, Major R. P. Davidson, of the Illinois National Guard, had built a machine-gun-armed motor-car, and similar experiments were being made all over Europe. The addition of armoured plate followed quickly. A boat-shaped 'war car', encased in a steel 'skirt' with chain mail brushing the ground, was exhibited at the Crystal Palace in 1902, and the following year became the first armoured fighting vehicle with rotating turrets. The armament was two Maxims, and the driver, the third member of the crew, steered by the aid of a periscope. The weight, however, was too much for the 15-horse-power Daimler engine, and the project never received official support. By 1914, engine and chassis design had advanced considerably, and 100 Rolls-Royce cars were purchased by the Admiralty, to provide armoured-car patrols for the Royal Naval Air Service squadrons based at Dunkirk. Initially, no

Rolls-Royce armoured car

overhead protection was provided for the crew, but in later versions, the Maxim gun was mounted in a revolving turret, and the crew of three or four men were 'boxed in' with ·3-inch armour plate. After the loss of Antwerp and Ostend, late in 1914, the armoured-car squadrons were sent out to West Africa and also saw service in many parts of the Middle East.

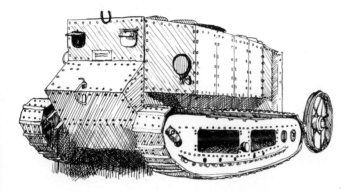

'Little Willie'; the first tank

THE TANK

To name the inventor of the tank should be easy. In 1912, L. E. de Mole, an Australian, sent to the War Office a design for an armoured fighting vehicle with true cross-country potential, but the plans went into a pigeon-hole, and nothing was done. Three years later, Mole, now a corporal in the Australian infantry, re-submitted his design, but production had already started on a tracked vehicle which eventually emerged as the first tank to be seen on any battlefield. After the war Mole's design was officially recognised as being superior in a number of respects. Fortunately, the problems arising from the deadlock of trench warfare were clearly seen by a few men of imagination who didn't use pigeon-holes. Winston Churchill, while First Lord of the Admiralty, had created the Armoured Car Force, and now set up a Landship Committee and personally followed up any idea, such as the use of enormous wheels or caterpillar tractors, that might negotiate the obstacles of the modern battlefield. It

209

'Mother'; a Mark 1 tank crossing a trench

was, however, an officer of the Royal Engineers, Lieutenant-Colonel E. D. Swinton, later Major-General Sir Ernest Swinton, who saw quite clearly that the solution to the problem posed by barbed-wire trenches and machine guns was an armed and armoured vehicle on tracks. Recalling a pre-war report on caterpillar tractors, used in America for agricultural purposes, Swinton persuaded the authorities to obtain several Holt tractors. Later, a kind of motorised steam roller called the Killen-Straight tractor was successfully demonstrated and, when fitted with an armoured car body in June, 1915, became the first tracked and armoured vehicle. Meanwhile, Swinton had produced a detailed plan for the employment of what he termed 'armoured machine gun destroyers' which, according to his calculations, would meet the War Office requirement of a vehicle that would cross a five-foot trench and climb a vertical four-and-a-half-foot parapet. Construction now went ahead at Foster's Engineering Works in Lincoln under the direction of William Tritton and Lieutenant W. G. Wilson of the Royal Naval Air Service. The Tritton tank was completed in September, 1915, becoming known as 'Little Willie'. The track frame was twelve feet long and there were two rear wheels which assisted in steering. 'Little Willie' had a crew of five and the intention was to mount a 6-pound

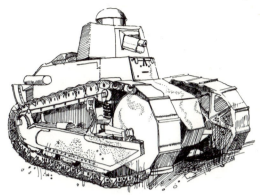

French Renault F T light tank

gun in a turret, but before the trials were complete, Wilson had developed a new design incorporating a brilliant and highly original idea. This was to carry the tracks right round the overall height of the vehicle to form a rhomboid which would considerably improve the tank's capacity to cross trenches. To lower the centre of gravity the turret was given up, and a 6-pounder gun was mounted in a sponson on both sides of the tank. The prototype was ready by the end of the year, and in January, 1916, 'Mother', as she was affectionately dubbed, was taken to Hatfield for a series of demonstrations before a number of Ministers and service representatives. 'Mother' exceeded all expectations, surmounting each obstacle with evident ease, and finished up by crossing a nine-foot trench. Within a few months production on 105 Mark 1 tanks had started; half were 'male' tanks, retaining the original 6-pounders as their main armament; the remainder which only mounted machine guns were known as 'female' tanks. Quite independently, due to the initiative of General Jean-Baptiste-Eugene Estienne, similar experimental work was going on in France. The original design, made in the Schneider Creusot works, amounted to an armoured box on a tractor chassis with a forward-mounted field gun as the main armament. Four hundred were ordered but none went into battle until April, 1917. They were used almost exclusively as mobile artillery. The French later concentrated on the Renault FT light tank. Details of the principal tanks used in the Great War are given in the table on pages 214 and 215.

15 SEPTEMBER 1916

Great secrecy surrounded the manufacture of the first tanks, which were so-named simply because their shape resembled that of the petrol tank on a popular make of motorcycle. By mid-August, 1916, at the height of the Battle of the Somme, sixty tanks had reached France. Douglas Haig, the British Commander-in-Chief, decided to use them immediately in his next big attack in the Flers-Courcelette sector. The main attack was to be made by the Fourth Army on a five-mile front after a three-day bombardment by over 1,250 guns, and the majority of the forty-nine fully operational tanks were allotted to this attack. A number of tanks ran into difficulties moving up overnight across the shell-pocked ground and when the attack started in the half light early on 15 September, only thirty-two left their starting points. These had been split up in penny packets between the divisions and now moved off through lanes left in the barrage some fifteen minutes ahead of the infantry. Nearly half the tanks broke down or got ditched and not all the remainder succeeded in reaching the objectives ahead of the infantry. The sight of even a few of these monstrous machines emerging through the mist and crashing through the wire, however, was altogether too much for some of the defenders who turned and bolted. In the centre of the sector a group of three tanks reached the village of Flers, which was nearly a mile from the starting point, and set about destroying machine-gun posts and breaking into fortified houses. Many of the defenders fled in panic and with the arrival of the infantry, the whole village was

Scene in the High Street of Flers

quickly cleared. The press reported this action in vivid terms: 'A tank is walking up the High Street of Flers with the British Army cheering behind'. Few soldiers, however, understood the true significance of this momentary glimpse of the coming revolution in warfare. Haig sent a request to the War Office for 1,000 tanks but it was to be fourteen months before the first massed tank attack was to take place. The policy of using tanks in penny packets continued and in the disastrous four-month struggle at Passchendaele, the newly formed Tank Corps nearly sank to oblivion like their vehicles in the swamp-like battlefield, and a constant war had to be waged against the apathy, incredulity, and short-sightedness of General Headquarters. Infantry, tanks, artillery and aircraft had to learn to work together. New tactics had to be evolved. Two British officers, Major Giffard Le Quesne Martel and Major Frederick Charles Fuller, both destined to rise to high rank in the army, became the advocates of armoured warfare. It was Fuller who wrote, 'Success in war depends upon mobility and mobility on time . . . the tank is first of all a time-saving machine, secondly a shield—it is, in fact, an armoured mechanical horse'. The tactics that were proposed were always based on surprise. For the coming spring offensive in 1917, Fuller recommended a separate echelon of tanks for

Name	Number produced to December, 1918		Thick-ness of plate (mm)	Weight in fighting trim (tons)	Over-all length (ft)	Engine	Miles per gallon of fuel
British Tank Mk I	Male Female	75 of each	8	26	26′	6 cyl. Daimler 105 h.p.	$\frac{1}{2}$
Tank Mk IV	Male Female	420 595	12	28	26′	as above	$\frac{1}{2}$
Tank Mk V	Male Female	200 200	12–14	29	26′	6 cyl. Ricardo 150 h.p.	$\frac{1}{2}$
Medium A 'Whippet'	200		12–14	14	20′	2 × 45 h.p. Tyler	1
'Liberty' (joint Anglo–American)	Pilot models only		12–16	37	34′	300 h.p. Liberty (Aero engine converted)	$\frac{1}{4}$
French Schneider	400		8–24	14·9	19′8″	6 cyl. Schneider 70 h.p.	$\frac{1}{2}$
St. Chamond	400		8–16	25	25′10″	4 cyl. Panhard 90 h.p.	$\frac{1}{2}$
Renault FT	over 3,000		16–22	7·4	16′5″	4 cyl. Renault 40 h.p.	1
German A7V	20		15–30	33	24′	2 × 4 cyl. Mercedes– Daimler 150 h.p.	$\frac{1}{2}$

Total production of tanks during the 1914–18 war: Britain 2,636;

France 3,870 mostly Renault light tanks; Germany 20.

adius on e fill in iles)	Armament		Max. speed m.p.h.	Gap crossed (ft)	Vertical obstacle climbed (ft)	Crew	
	Gun	MGs					
23	2 × 6 pr —	+3 5	4	10'	6'	8	Production started February, 1916. First tanks in action ever, 15 September, 1916
33	as above		4	10'	6'	8	Production started February, 1917. In action June, 1917. Also 100 Marks II and III—like Mark I, but not tails
45	as above		5	10'	6'	8	Production started December, 1917. In action July, 1918
80	—	2	9	7'	4'	3	Production started December, 1917. In action March, 1918 and at Battle of Amiens
55	2 × 6 pr	+7*	5½	14'	6'	8	Initial order 1,500 from new factory in France, plus many more from Britain and America—production stopped by Armistice
25	75 mm (short)	+2	5	5' 10"	2' 7"	6	Production started February, 1916. In action April, 1917. Then used as assault artillery
37	75 mm	+4	5	8'	15"	9	Production started April, 1916. In action May, 1917. Used as assault artillery
24	37 mm or	1	6	5' (7' with tail)	2' 3"	2	Production started late 1916. In action May, 1918
25	57 mm	+6	8	6	1' 6"	18	Production started 1918, 100 ordered. Only 20 tanks completed. Some others used as cargo carriers

* (Three manned simultaneously)

the assault of each successive defence line and said that no bombardment should last more than forty-eight hours, but the High Command wouldn't listen. The artillery officer who supported Fuller was promoted out of the way, and the bombardment increased to four days, preceded by seventeen days of shelling to cut the wire entanglements in front of the German trenches.

THE BATTLE OF CAMBRAI, NOVEMBER 1917

The French town of Cambrai lay just behind the Hindenburg Line, and the Germans considered that this particular sector was impregnable. All three defence lines lay along the reverse slopes of low ridges, and were completely hidden from British artillery observers. The trenches were twelve feet across and eighteen feet deep, and had a high parapet and parados, so shaped as to increase the gap to as much as eighteen feet across. The wire entanglements were at least fifty yards deep and covered by innumerable machine-gun posts. Very deep concrete shelters allowed the troops to live in comfort completely immune from anything but a direct hit from the heaviest shell. The dry, bare and rolling chalk plateau leading up to the position, however, was ideal tank country and Fuller had twice proposed a major tank raid of a few hours' duration in the sector, some six to eight miles wide, that lay between two canals opposite Cambrai. The Germans, who estimated that it would take the Allies five weeks to cut the wire entanglements by shell fire, held this particular section of the line with only two divisions and 150 guns. As it happened, on the day of the battle a relief division was also in the line. The British attack had now been prepared as a full-scale operation by eight divisions supported by 1,000 guns and 300 aircraft. Three more divisions and a cavalry division stood by in reserve. A total of 476 tanks were allocated, 54 of which were in

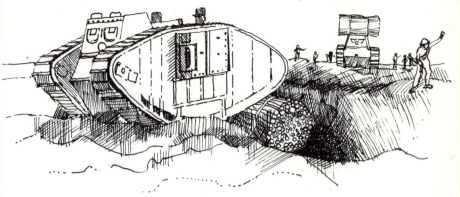

Tanks at the battle of Cambrai

'mechanical reserve' and a further 98 were given special tasks, such as carrying supplies or enlarging gaps in the wire with heavy grapnels. The 324 fighting tanks for the assault were all Mark IVs. To enable them to cross the very wide trenches, each carried on its nose an enormous fascine made out of brushwood, which weighed one and three-quarter tons, with a special release gear so that it could be toppled into a trench. This would enable each section of three tanks to cross the three successive barriers. The tactics employed were utterly different from those of earlier attacks. Well before dawn the tanks were spread out on a six-mile front. The move forward had been done so quietly that many of the infantry were quite unaware that the tanks had already formed up during the night. Major General Hugh Elles, the Tank Corps commander, had posted himself in the centre of the line, and at 6:10 A.M., in dense ground mist, both the tanks and the infantry moved forward together. Ten minutes later, as the sky began to lighten, the barrage crashed down on the German outpost line. The leading 'advance guard' tanks were now only 250 yards short of their first objectives and opened fire on the German positions to keep the defenders' heads down. A little way behind came the 'main body' tanks, closely followed by sections

217

of infantry in single file. Captain D. G. Browne later wrote:

'The German outposts, dazed or annihilated by the sudden deluge of shells, were overrun in an instant. The triple belts of wire were crossed as if they had been beds of nettles . . . The defenders of the front trench, scrambling out of dug-outs and shelters to meet the crash and flame of the barrage, saw the leading tanks almost upon them, their appearance made the more grotesque and terrifying by the huge black bundles they carried on their cabs.'

In a little over four hours, the main defences of the formidable Hindenburg Line had been overrun, but the troops were exhausted, 179 tanks had been hit or disabled in various ways, and many needed repair; the strain on the crews had been very great and they all needed rest. Through insufficient reserves, and in the growing darkness, the decision was taken not to order the cavalry forward. By the next day it was too late, and in the subsequent fighting, the Germans recovered almost as much ground as had been captured in the first few hours of the battle. There could no longer be any doubt, however, of what tanks could achieve when the principles of concentration and surprise were applied in their use, and the Battle of Cambrai changed the tactical climate of the war—and of warfare.

CONCLUSION

When the Armistice came in 1918 fighter aircraft were flying at over 150 miles per hour, had a ceiling of 25,000 feet, and could climb to 10,000 feet in ten minutes. Britain's Independent Bomber Force included four-engined Handley Page aircraft with a bomb load of 7,500 pounds and a radius of action of 1,300 miles. Germany was building 'Giant' biplanes (which stood 140 feet high and weighed twelve tons) and had designed K-Wagen 'landships' weighing 148 tons and with a crew of eighteen. Martel's concept of 'sea warfare on

218

land', moreover, had inspired 'Plan 1919' in which an Allied 'Tank Army' of 5,000 tanks would gain victory by a deep and swift 'penetration' of sixty miles in six days. Here, then, with the return of armour in land warfare we end this account of men and inventions that have shaped the destiny of many nations and of Western civilisation over three centuries, from the age of gunpowder to the age of oil.

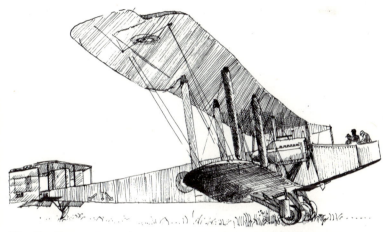

Handley Page twin-engined bomber of the British Independent Bomber Force

GLOSSARY

Accoutrements: a soldier's equipment other than his arms and dress.

Arms Drill: drill movements to practise the soldier in handling his personal weapons.

Arquebus: a shoulder gun fired from a forked rest.

Basinet: a small light steel helmet.

Bastion: a fortified work built at the angle made by the ramparts of a fort.

219

Bazooka: a portable anti-tank rocket launcher.

Block Trail: a gun trail ending in a single beam.

Blunderbuss: a short shoulder gun with a large bore, firing many balls.

Butt Box: a compartment in the butt of a rifle to hold patches and small tools.

Calibre: the internal diameter or 'bore' of a gun.

Carbine: a short musket or rifle used by cavalry.

Case-shot: an artillery projectile consisting of a canister containing bullets or musket balls.

Charge (gun): explosive which propels the projectile.

Chemin de rondes: a walk going all round the fort along the rampart.

Clinometer: an instrument for measuring slopes and elevations.

Courtine: the long straight front of the rampart between two bastions.

Cuirass: body armour reaching to the waist, consisting of a breast-plate and a back-plate buckled together.

Demi-lune: a detached triangular work built in the moat of a fort.

Fascine: a long cylindrical bundle of brushwood firmly bound together used in filling ditches, etc.

Flint-lock: a gun lock using a flint to strike against steel to produce sparks which ignite the priming powder.

Fougasse: a type of small land mine, often charged with a loaded shell.

Fulminate: a compound of fulminic acid with a base which detonates by percussion, friction or heat.

Fuse: a tube containing combustible material by which a shell is ignited and exploded.

Fusil, also Fuzee: a light musket.

Glacis: the ground sloping away from the top of the parapet of a fort towards the open country.

Gorget: a piece of armour to protect the throat.

Grape-shot: an artillery projectile consisting of a canister filled with small pellets.

Grapnel: a device with iron claws, attached to a rope or chain, used for dragging.

Grenade: a small container, usually of metal, filled with explosive and thrown by hand.

Halberd: a weapon combining spear and battle-axe.

Hanger: a short sword, originally 'hung' from the belt.

Hollow-square: a formation adopted by infantry so as to defend themselves from attack from any direction.

Hornwork: a detached fortified work outside a fort.

Jaeger: a German (or Swiss) huntsman, hence a rifleman in a German corps.

Janizary: a Turkish soldier.

Képi: a French military cap with a flat top and peak.

Kukri: a curved knife used by Gurkhas.

Limber: the detachable front portion of a gun carriage.

Magazine: a storage place for arms, ammunition and provisions. Also a receptacle for cartridges that are fed into the breech of a rifle or machine gun.

Mameluke: a member of a mounted military force in the service of a Moslem ruler or caliph.

Matchlock: a gun lock in which a slow-match is used for igniting the powder.

Matrose: a gunner's assistant, or mate, in a train of artillery.

Musquettoon: a short musket with a large bore.

Palisade: defences made from strong posts set in rows.

Parados: an earthwork to protect the rear of a trench.

Parapet: a defence work of earth, or stone, along the front of a trench or along the top of a rampart.

Partizan: a long-handled spear with cutting projections on the blade.

Percussion Cap: a small container filled with fulminate which, when struck, fires an explosive charge.

Phalanx: a body of heavily-armed infantry in close order.

Pike: a weapon with a long wooden shaft and a pointed iron or steel head.

Priming Powder: an explosive compound used to fire the charge of a gun.

Pyrite: a metallic compound that gives off sparks when struck with steel.

Quillon: the two arms that form the cross-guard of a sword or dagger.

Recuperator: a device for returning an artillery piece to its normal position after the buffer has taken the shock of recoil.

Redoubt: a detached field work, usually rectangular in shape.

Shako: a tall military cap with a peak and a broad top surmounted by a plume or 'pom-pom'.

Shell: a projectile filled with explosive.

Shot: a solid projectile.

Skirmishers: soldiers who move in loose order ahead of the main body.

Sponson: a gun platform standing out from the side of a vessel or a tank.

Targe: a light shield or buckler.

Tenaille: a detached oblong work built in the moat of a fort.

Tirailleur: a rifleman or sharpshooter.

Traverse (in a trench system): an earth barrier at intervals to prevent enfilade fire.

Trunnion: the round projection or 'gudgeon' on either side of a cannon by which it is pivoted on its carriage.

Tuck: a straight pointed thrusting sword.

Uhlan: a lancer, originally recruited from Poland.

Volley Fire: simultaneous discharge of many missiles.

Zouave: a French light infantryman recruited in Algeria.

Index